CREATING EMOTIONALLY LITERATE CLASSROOMS:

AN INTRODUCTION TO THE RULER APPROACH TO SOCIAL AND EMOTIONAL LEARNING

Edited by
Marc A. Brackett
and
Janet Pickard Kremenitzer

WITH
Marvin Maurer
Susan E. Rivers
Nicole A. Elbertson
Marilyn D. Carpenter

Foreword by Peter Salovey,
Provost and Chris Argyris Professor of Psychology, Yale University

DUDE PUBLISHING
A Division of
National Professional Resources, Inc.
www.NPRinc.com

Printed in the United States of America

ISBN 978-1-934032-18-3

PUBLISHING
A Division of:
National Professional Resources, Inc.
Corporate: Katonah, NY
Operations: Naples, FL

For information:
National Professional Resources, Inc.
1455 Rail Head Blvd., Suite 6
Naples, FL 34110
www.NPRinc.com
Toll Free: (800) 453-7461

Acquisitions Editor: Helene M. Hanson
Associate Editor: Lisa L. Hanson
Production Editor, Cover Design: Andrea Cerone

Table of Contents

Acknowledgements

We would like to extend our gratitude to the many individuals and groups who helped make this book a success. We especially wish to thank David Caruso, James Casey, Laura Castro, Michelle Cook, Edward Fale, Chris Gerry, Thomas Hecht, Ashley Hines, Allison Holzer, Amy Latimer, Peggy Lewis, Clare Lloyd, Paulo Lopes, Jack Mayer, Regina Miller, Sarah Minkus, Justyna Mojsa, Kathy Neuhaus, Raquel Palomera-Martin, Janet Patti, Peter Salovey, Caroline Seligman, Kristina Schmid, Robin Stern, Linda Wanosky, Roger Weissberg, Melanie Wilson, Edward Zigler, and the members of the Health, Emotion, and Behavior Laboratory at Yale University, all of whom discussed with us the ideas presented in this book and read early drafts of the chapters. Their feedback was invaluable, and we greatly appreciate their goodwill and patience. We also wish to express our appreciation for the numerous gifted teachers and administrators from the Valley Stream, Brewster, and South Orangetown school districts in New York; the Hartford and Middletown school districts in Connecticut; Amistad Academy in New Haven; New Line Learning Academy of Kent, England; and the Catholic Schools of Brooklyn and Queens, New York. These educators contributed significantly to our thinking and therefore to the content of each chapter. Finally, we wish to thank the William T. Grant Foundation and the Institution for Social and Policy Studies at Yale University for providing us with the support and funding necessary to continuously enhance our programs. Janet would also like to acknowledge, in loving memory, her mother, Francine Pickard, and in honor of her father, Leonard. The editors would also like to express appreciation to the staff of their publisher, particularly Helene Hanson and Andrea Cerone.

Foreword

I am honored to contribute these opening words to *Creating Emotionally Literate Classrooms,* not simply because Marc Brackett and his team are affiliated with the Health, Emotion, and Behavior Laboratory at Yale University (which I direct), but because The RULER Approach represents the most comprehensive, research-based, social and emotional learning (SEL) program in the emotional intelligence field. I'm not surprised, of course, as The RULER Approach is the result of a collaboration of researchers and educators, and its programs have been field-tested in and adopted by diverse school systems.

It is important to note that the ideas for teaching emotional literacy in the ways presented in this book were first developed by Marvin Maurer and influenced by his several decades of teaching experience. These foundational ideas were then synthesized with research by Marc Brackett, and Janet Pickard Kremenitzer and Susan Rivers, among others, concerning the development of emotional competencies in children and teachers. The result is a program which is both well grounded in science and can be put into practice in any school. The RULER Approach differs from many other SEL programs: it is supported by research, was developed with an eye toward implementation in real world school systems, and integrates cutting-edge affective science with wisdom derived from years of experience in the classroom.

The role of emotional literacy in the developing child is similar to that of traditional, analytic intelligence. Emotions constitute a unique source of information for individuals about their surrounding environment and prospects, and this information informs their thoughts, actions, and subsequent feelings. Emotional literacy represents the knowledge that gives rise to a set of interrelated competencies which allows children to process emotionally relevant information more efficiently and accurately.

The RULER Approach is organized around a helpful mnemonic, RULER, which stands for *Recognizing, Understanding, Labeling, Expressing,* and *Regulating emotion*—the core skills in developing emotional competence. Children differ in how skilled they are emotionally, and their level of emotional literacy contributes substantially to their intellectual, social, and emotional well-being and growth.

I am enthusiastic about the work presented in *Creating Emotionally Literate Classrooms* and hope educators will consider adopting The RULER Approach for use in their classrooms and schools. However, I should conclude on a cautionary note. Rather than a panacea for all developmental problems, emotional literacy is a set of competencies that can be used in prosocial or antisocial ways. Simply developing children's emotional literacy may not prove sufficient unless the contextual and motivational factors affecting the use of these skills is also addressed. Programs that offer the possibilities of ameliorating major school-based problems, from obesity to substance abuse to teen pregnancy to violence, but that do not address contextual features of schools, are misguided. And, that's where the learning contexts created by school leaders and teachers are critically important. The developers of The RULER Approach fully acknowledge the importance of learning contexts and the training programs help school leaders and teachers create supportive and empowering settings so that students thrive and can develop their RULER skills. In that sense, school leaders and teachers can partner with the developers of this approach to work in the best interests of students.

Peter Salovey
Yale University
New Haven, CT

Teacher's Commentary

When I finished the requirements to become a teacher, I was given my first job as a sixth grade social studies teacher in a small, rural community in upstate New York. After teaching for a while, I began to enter the classroom with guarded enthusiasm. I had the realization that my students were not reaching their fullest potential. Then, one day, one of my students stood up in class and asked a question. We had just finished a rather boring discussion of dates, names, and places they were to memorize for a test. The student asked, "Mr. Maurer, honestly, what does all this stuff have to do with everyday life?" Suddenly, I became the student. I was stunned, not only by his courage, but by the fact that he realized that we weren't really "making it" as a class. I replied instantly by praising him for having the courage to ask such an important question and promising him that I would think about the question and give an answer to him and the class soon.

I went home that night and pondered the simple question my student asked. This may have led to one of the most important lessons I ever learned as a teacher. It was a great epiphany: How can any teacher expect young students to learn or memorize dates, names, and places of things that occurred well before they were conceived? How can children be expected to absorb information that is completely unrelated to their real, everyday world—their social and emotional lives?

I kept searching for a method that would help students "connect" what I was obligated to teach, such as historic events dating back to Ancient Greece, to their day-to-day personal experiences. I began to think that the missing link had something to do with their emotions and feelings. However, this was in the early 1970s, and words such as emotional literacy and emotional intelligence had not yet entered the academic lexicon or educational community in any popular way.

I was therefore left to my own devices to create a way to elicit these connections in the classroom. Many times I felt like the Wright Brothers must have felt when they investigated flight—I knew something existed that could make learning more meaningful, but I had no actual proof of it. After much soul searching and a great deal of research, I came up with a simple question that ultimately had a simple answer: What is the common human experience that historical figures and my students have in common? My answer was feelings.

As promised, I entered my classroom a few weeks later with a new, unguarded enthusiasm, telling my students that because of them, I had come up with something that I believed would help them learn. This "something" would make it easier not only to learn the history curriculum, but also to learn something about themselves. I began to develop a new approach to teaching history. As you might anticipate, my approach used the language of feelings. I started integrating a list of feeling words that conveyed to the students what some prominent historical figures most likely had in common with them in their present day lives. I also started introducing lessons by having my students identify with the feelings and emotions of people in history. For example, before teaching about the Roman oligarchy, I had my students brainstorm about what it would feel like to be on a team with four captains. They discussed how the team would function and the feelings associated with having multiple leaders. Students engaged in heated discussions about the benefits and problems of this leadership structure, readily comparing and contrasting the situation they were conceiving of in present day with that described in their history books.

Because it was the 1970s and there wasn't much of a precedent for this style of teaching, my methods quickly became the target of gossip in the teachers' lounge. Soon, my very worried social studies coordinator approached me at a staff meeting. He said, "Maurer, you've been critical of our current curriculum since you began teaching here, and I can no longer defend your renegade ways of teaching. I have a proposition for you: stop complaining and write a real curriculum. Over the summer, write something that both encompasses what your classroom experience is telling you and addresses what we need to get across for the state requirements. If it's good, I will fight the system to let you teach it next year." I took the challenge without knowing anything about how to write a "real" curriculum.

I had been writing a column for the weekly newspaper entitled, "Are We Doing the Best for Our Children?" and I realized this could serve as a great foundation for my 'unwritten' curriculum. That summer, I began to compile information that would later be developed into the first version of our emotional literacy program, *The Feeling Words Curriculum,* which was the precursor to the approach to social and emotional learning that is presented in this book.

After reviewing my work, the coordinator decided that I could, in fact, begin to teach using these new methods. My students immediately rose to the challenges I gave them. Participation in class increased dramatically; students remembered historical events with no prompting; and they tested better than any other sixth grade social studies class in the district.

I taught using these methods until I retired in 1990. At that time, I put the *Feeling Words Curriculum* on a shelf in my home office where it remained for about eight years. Then, one day, my nephew and now colleague, Marc Brackett, approached me about bringing the *Feeling Words Curriculum* back to life. At that time, Marc had just finished his first master's degree in forensic psychology and was preparing applications for various doctoral programs in psychology. He alerted me to the world's newfound fascination with emotional intelligence—an area of research in which Marc would eventually became a leading expert, trained by both co-founders of the theory, Peter Salovey and Jack Mayer.

Marc and I began a series of long conversations about what I had done as a teacher and the plan he was embarking on as an academic psychologist. Together, we developed a way to marry my teaching methods with his scientific knowledge and expertise on the role of emotions and emotional skills in learning, well-being, and social competence. We inspired each other and decided to work together to produce our first emotional literacy curriculum for middle school students. That curriculum, which has been shown experimentally to increase academic achievement and social competence, is now being used in schools throughout the United States and abroad. What you are about to read is an introduction to the emotional literacy curriculum. It represents the collective expertise of many of our colleagues—gifted researchers, administrators, and teachers—who have worked with us to develop The RULER Approach to social and emotional learning.

This way of teaching has been a passion of mine for over 30 years. When I retired twenty one years ago, I never expected to be working on and thinking about emotional literacy as critically as I am today. What began as a way for me to teach students about ancient societies has become a way to provide students with a solid foundation upon which they can feel secure in school, enjoy learning, build literacy skills, and interact successfully with their peers, teachers, and family members. This program is for our students so they can reach their fullest potential. They deserve the best we can give them.

Marvin Maurer
Vestal, New York

Preface

Emotional literacy—which includes the knowledge and skills associated with Recognizing, Understanding, Labeling, Expressing, and Regulating emotion (RULER)—is vital to effective teaching, successful academic performance, and quality relationships.[1-4] Teachers with high emotional literacy, for example, experience more positive emotions in the classroom, receive more support from co-workers, employ more effective coping strategies during stressful encounters, and report less burnout and greater job satisfaction than their less emotionally literate counterparts. Students of emotionally literate teachers have been found to enjoy learning in their classrooms.[5] Emotionally literate students flourish as well. They have positive attitudes toward school and their teachers, are self-reliant, have better-quality interpersonal relationships, and experience fewer negative emotional symptoms (e.g., stress, anxiety, and depression). Teachers also describe emotionally literate students as being less hyperactive, aggressive, anxious and depressed; having fewer school problems and behavioral symptoms; and possessing better social skills, study skills, and leadership potential than students who lack emotional literacy.[6]

Research shows that a common element among schools that report an increase in academic success, better teacher-student relationships, and a decrease in problem behavior is the presence of a systematic process for promoting emotional literacy, or, more broadly, social and emotional learning (SEL).[7] The evidence is so convincing that states such as Illinois and Alaska have created learning standards for SEL, similar to learning standards for math, writing, and reading.

In order for SEL programs to be successful, they must meet a number of criteria. The Collaborative for Academic, Social, and Emotional Learning (CASEL) provides researchers, educators, and policy makers with guidance on how to develop school-based SEL programs. CASEL recommends that schools select SEL programs that are based on sound psychological or educational theory, are field-tested, and are shown to be effective through scientific evaluation.[8,9] To integrate SEL programs effectively into schools, CASEL recommends that schools train both teachers and students on social and emotional skills. Effective integration also requires support from all levels of the district, including the superintendent, school board, principals, and teachers.

The RULER Approach is a theoretically based, field-tested program that adheres to CASEL's standards. It was designed by psychologists, teachers, educators of teachers, school administrators, and students to advance the general mission of schools: to educate the whole child. The program achieves this goal by:
- Offering school administrators and educators training and support to develop their own emotional literacy and implement the program effectively;
- Providing developmentally and culturally appropriate instruction for students;
- Helping to create a caring and engaging learning environment;
- Teaching students to apply emotional literacy both in and outside of school;

- Enhancing school performance by addressing the cognitive, emotional, and social dimensions of learning;
- Encouraging school-home partnerships; and
- Including opportunities for continuous evaluation and improvement through coaching and systematic monitoring.

The RULER Approach is grounded in the RULER model of emotional literacy,[10] which is based on decades of research on emotional intelligence and emotional development.[11] This model asserts that personal, social, and intellectual functioning improves by teaching students and educators the knowledge associated with Recognizing, Understanding, Labeling, Expressing, and Regulating emotions. Students learn about RULER through numerous interactive and engaging activities such as self-reflection, analysis of academic material and current events, family conversations, symbolic representations of emotion terms, classroom discussions, and creative writing. The program enhances social and emotional development by promoting self-awareness, empathy, communication skills, healthy relationships, and better decision making. It also promotes academic success by enhancing students' vocabulary, comprehension, writing, creativity, and critical thinking. In these ways, emotional literacy helps schools meet national and state educational goals.

A recent field evaluation conducted by the Health, Emotion, and Behavior Laboratory at Yale University supports the power of emotional literacy training. In the study, fifth and sixth grade classrooms across three schools were randomly assigned to receive either emotional literacy training or the school's standard character education program. After just seven months, students who received emotional literacy training earned higher end-of-the-year grades in writing, reading, social studies, and science than students who received the standard character education program. Students trained in emotional literacy also had higher grades in social development and work habits. They were more likely to complete their homework, work cooperatively with others, demonstrate self-control, and pay attention to the rules of the classroom and the school.[12]

This book is an overview of The RULER Approach. We have program offerings for students in kindergarten through eighth grade, teachers across these grade levels, and for administrators (see www.therulerapproach.org for more information).[13-15] To date, schools throughout the United States, including New York, New Jersey, Connecticut, Michigan, and Arkansas, as well as in districts throughout England, have adopted these programs. In addition to the positive results from the evaluations, feedback from the stakeholders involved in the programs, including administrators, teachers, counselors, parents, and students, shows that the programs are well-received, enjoyable, and produce quantifiable benefits. Teachers, principals, and superintendents report having improved relationships with colleagues, parents, and students. Students enjoy emotional literacy because it addresses them as individuals, including their specific social, emotional, and academic needs. In particular, students participating in this program tell us that they feel more secure expressing themselves without the fear of being judged and criticized, and have a better understanding of their peers and family members. Teachers tell us that when they teach emotional literacy in their classrooms, students interact more effectively with peers with whom they previously were unable to maintain positive interactions, demonstrate less problem behavior and more prosocial behavior, write better, and incorporate feeling words into other curriculum areas. Teachers also report having more positive relationships with their students, feeling more comfortable sharing their own emotions and experiences with their students, having a better ability to recognize and respond constructively to students' social and emotional needs, and having a keener awareness of their own and their students' emotions and how emotions contribute to the maintenance of a healthy classroom climate.

The RULER Approach brings the emotional and social lives of teachers and students into the classroom, treating some of the most important aspects of the day as relevant and integral to learning. Emotional literacy provides a foundation for students' successful cognitive, social, emotional, and behavior development, which enables schools to make a genuine commitment to supporting the holistic development of their students.

Overview of This Book

The first three chapters present an overview of The RULER Approach to social and emotional learning (SEL). *Chapter 1, Creating Emotionally Literate Learning Communities,* introduces the classroom program, *Emotional Literacy for Students.* Teachers can embed the tools and lessons of *Emotional Literacy for Students* into regular classroom instruction from elementary to middle school. This program is designed to both create emotionally literate learning environments and develop in students a core set of skills that help them to be more engaged and successful in learning, have mutually supportive relationships, and make healthy decisions. *Chapter 2, The Feeling Words Curriculum,* provides an overview of the program and describes how teachers regularly integrate emotional literacy lessons into their English language arts, social studies, health, and other subject areas. The program is engaging for both teachers and students and strengthens student learning across the curriculum. *Chapter 3, Emotionally Literate Teaching,* describes a training program that offers educators an opportunity to develop their emotional literacy and apply these skills in the school environment. Brackett and colleagues discuss the relevance of attending to and using emotions in the classroom, and provide sample tools and exercises. For example, the *Blueprint* is one tool that helps teachers and students effectively cope with and respond to past, present and future emotional experiences and challenging situations. This chapter also includes activities for reflective practice to increase emotional literacy and effectiveness as a teacher.

The last two chapters include a research overview of the importance of emotional literacy for student development, as well as implementation guidelines. *Chapter 4, Educating the Whole Child with Emotional Literacy: Links to Social, Emotional, and Academic Competence,* outlines the need for emotional literacy in schools and the ways in which The RULER Approach helps schools both achieve academic goals set by national and state standards and prepare students for life inside and outside of the classroom. Rivers and colleagues describe several ways in which The RULER Approach, and the classroom program in particular, contributes to student success. For example, the Feeling Words Curriculum is structured to foster individualized and integrated learning, encourage and support school-home partnerships, and incorporate multiple modes of instruction to address the various learning needs of all students. This structure promotes student learning, well-being, and confidence (both academic and social) by enhancing the supportive and caring features of the classroom environment, helping students develop critical thinking skills and a sense of empowerment in their academic and social lives, and encouraging empathic understanding.

Finally, Chapter 5, Integrating The RULER Approach into your School: Guidelines for Effective Implementation of the Student Programs, provides recommendations for ensuring successful implementation. In this chapter, Elbertson and colleagues identify three critical phases of implementation. First, schools need to secure commitments from key stakeholders, including teachers, parents, the superintendent, and other administrators. To prepare for implementation, schools should take steps such as appointing a project coordinator, creating a committee to manage implementation, identifying and allocating resources for the program (such as funds for training and teachers for instructing the program), scheduling teacher trainings, and establishing a process for teacher support. This chapter provides recommendations for evaluating the quality of program implementation and its impact on students and the school as a whole. Adhering to the guidelines set forth in this chapter will help schools ensure that The RULER Approach is well integrated and achieves the intended results.

References: Preface

1. Brackett, M. A., & Salovey, P. (2004). Measuring emotional intelligence with the Mayer-Salovey-Caruso Emotional Intelligence Test (MSCEIT). In G. Geher (Ed.), *Measuring emotional intelligence: Common ground and controversy* (pp. 179-194). Happauge, NY: Nova Science Publishers, Inc.

2. Mayer, J. D., Salovey, P., & Caruso, D. R. (2004). Emotional intelligence: Theory, findings, and implications. *Psychological Inquiry,* 15(3), 197-215.

3. Greenberg, M. T., Weissberg, R. P., O'Brien, M. U., Zins, J. E., Fredericks, L., Resnik, H., et al. (2003). Enhancing school-based prevention and youth development through coordinated social, emotional, and academic learning. *American Psychologist,* 58, 466-474.

4. Sutton, R. E., & Wheatley, K. F. (2003). Teachers' emotions and teaching: A review of the literature and directions for future research. *Educational Psychology Review,* 15(4), 327-358.

5. Brackett, M. A., Palomera Martin, R., Mojsa, J., Reyes, M. R., & Salovey, P. (2010). Emotion regulation ability, job satisfaction, and burnout among British secondary school teachers. *Psychology in the Schools,* 47, 406-417.

6. Rivers, S. E., Brackett, M. A., Reyes, M. R., & Salovey, P. (2008). Emotion skills in early adolescence: Relationships to academic and social functioning, *Annual Meeting of the American Educational Research Association.* New York, NY.

7. Durlak, J. A., Weissberg, R. P., Dymnicki, A. B., Taylor, R. D., & Schellinger, K. B. (in press). The impact of enhancing students' social and emotional learning: A meta-analysis of school-based universal interventions. *Child Development.*

8. Elias, M. J., Zins, J. E., Weissberg, R. P., Frey, K. S., Greenberg, M. T., Haynes, N. M., et al. (1997). *Promoting social and emotional learning: Guidelines for educators.* Alexandria, VA: Association for Supervision and Curriculum Development.

9. Zins, J. E., Weissberg, R. P., Wang, M. C., & Walberg, H. J. (Eds.). (2004). *Building academic success on social and emotional learning: What does the research say?* New York: Teachers College Press.

10. Brackett, M. A., & Rivers, S. E. (2011). *The Missing Link: How Emotional Literacy Promotes Personal, Academic, and Social Success.* New York: Teachers College Press (forthcoming).

11. Mayer, J. D., Salovey, P., & Caruso, D. R. (2008). Emotional intelligence: New ability or eclectic traits? *American Psychologist,* 63, 503-517.

12. Brackett, M. A., Rivers, S. E., Reyes, M.R. & Salovey, P. (2010). Enhancing academic performance and social and emotional competence with The RULER feeling words curriculum. *Learning and Individual Differences.*

13. Maurer, M., & Brackett, M. A. (2004). *Emotional Literacy in the Middle School: A 6-step program to promote social, emotional, & academic learning.* Port Chester, NY: National Professional Resources.

14. Brackett, M. A., Caruso, D. R., Rivers, S. E., & Stern, R. (2009). *RULER for Families.* New Haven, CT: Emotionally Intelligent Schools.

15. Brackett, M. A., & Caruso, D. R. (2007). *Emotional literacy for administrators.* New Haven, CT: Emotionally Intelligent Schools.

Chapter 1
Creating Emotionally Literate Learning Environments

*Marc A. Brackett, Susan E. Rivers, Marvin Maurer, Nicole A. Elbertson,
and Janet Pickard Kremenitzer*

The RULER Approach to social and emotional learning (SEL) is a comprehensive, whole-school method for building the skills of recognizing, understanding, labeling, expressing, and regulating emotion ("RULER"), which are foundational to academic, social, and personal success. The RULER Approach changes the way school leaders, educators, students, and families think about emotions so they can leverage the power of emotions to enhance learning, social relationships, and well-being. This chapter presents an introduction to *Emotional Literacy for Students,* which are the learning tools and lessons that teachers embed into regular classroom instruction from elementary to middle school. The tools and lessons are designed to both create emotionally literate learning environments and develop in students a core set of skills that help them to be more engaged and successful in learning, have mutually supportive relationships, and make healthy decisions.

Teachers are central to the success of *Emotional Literacy for Students.* Teachers who begin using the RULER tools and emotional literacy lessons with their students soon observe positive results—for students as well as for themselves. Some teachers are hesitant initially to make emotions a focus in students' learning; upon embarking on the program they quickly realize that emotions are an integral part of learning.

The tools and strategies offered by The RULER Approach help teachers harness the value of emotions in ways that make learning more productive and engaging. Teachers who adopt *Emotional Literacy for Students* in their teaching participate in a series of professional development trainings to develop their own skills and teaching practices so that they are successful at creating supportive and empowering learning environments for students. Teachers initially work with coaches to help ensure the success of the program in their classrooms. Chapter 3, *Emotionally Literate Teaching,* provides an overview of *Emotional Literacy for Educators,* the professional development series that focuses on developing the skills of teachers and other educators in schools.

The cornerstone of *Emotional Literacy for Students* is the Feeling Words Curriculum for kindergarten through eighth grades. The Feeling Words Curriculum integrates a vocabulary of emotion into existing academic curricula using myriad pedagogical techniques designed to develop the intellectual, emotional, and social skills of students. The curriculum incorporates activities such as self-reflection, analysis of academic material and current events, artistic expression, family interactions, classroom discussions, and problem solving. Each activity motivates students to learn about their own feelings, take others' perspectives, become more engaged and successful in their school work, and develop supportive relationships. Across the activities, students acquire knowledge about RULER and practice using their RULER skills.

In the first section of this chapter, we provide an overview of emotional literacy and the RULER skills, highlighting the critical importance of each skill to achievements across the domains of students' lives. In the second section, we describe three of the RULER Anchor Tools—the Classroom Charter, the Mood Meter, and the Blueprint. These tools help teachers create positive, emotionally literate learning environments for students. Finally, in the third section we introduce the Feeling Words Curriculum, describe the importance of feelings words, and give an overview of its lessons and activities.

What is Emotional Literacy?

The RULER model of emotional literacy is derived from theoretical and empirical work on emotional intelligence.[1-4] It posits that teaching and providing opportunities to apply emotion knowledge is necessary to build relationships, promote healthy living, prevent problematic behavior, and increase academic achievement. This model includes five relatively distinct yet interrelated domains of emotion which have been identified by researchers as important for successful functioning and adaptation.[2-11] The acronym RULER refers to these five domains, which include:

Recognition of emotion. Recognizing that an emotion has occurred is the first clue that something important is happening in the environment. Recognition involves noticing a change reflective of an emotional experience that is present in one's own thoughts or body, or in someone else's words, facial expression, or behavior. Children who understand the emotional cues expressed by peers, teachers, and parents can modify their own behavior and respond in ways that are socially appropriate and helpful in achieving goals.[5,12]

Understanding emotion. Each emotion is triggered by different types of events and leads to relatively distinct patterns of thoughts and behaviors. Children with a deeper understanding of emotions know what causes emotions to occur, what they signify about their goals and well-being, what they feel like, and how emotions may influence their thoughts, decisions, and behavior.[13] When children understand emotions, they are better able to use effective problem-solving strategies to cope with negative and positive events.[14] Understanding emotions also enables children to interpret situations from others' perspectives and develop empathy.[7]

Labeling emotion. Labeling emotion refers to making connections between the experience of emotion and emotion-related words. Children with a sophisticated vocabulary to describe their emotions can differentiate between elation, satisfaction, and enthusiasm, and choose to use these terms as opposed to vague statements such as "I feel good." Accurately labeling emotions helps children communicate effectively with others, reducing misunderstanding in social interactions. Children who can label emotions properly have more positive social interactions, whereas children with deficits in labeling emotions display behavioral and learning problems.[15]

Expression of emotion. Expressing emotion refers to the communication of feelings, including the appropriate ways and times to express emotions and feelings. Children who have difficulty labeling and expressing emotions appropriately often are disconnected from others.[16] However, children who discuss their emotions with others at suitable times can ask for help with identifying strategies for dealing with emotions. If they are able to express themselves according to display rules (social norms for appropriate emotional behavior) they will be better received by others.[17] Moreover, expressing emotions in words has been shown to improve well-being and even physical health. Many studies shows that people who write about their emotions and the events that cause them are less likely to get sick than those who do not.[18]

Regulation of emotion. Regulating emotion refers to managing the thoughts, feelings, and behaviors that occur with an emotional experience.[6,7] When emotions are managed, they may be **p**revented (e.g., frustration avoided), **r**educed (e.g., rage lessened to annoyance), **i**nitiated (e.g., happiness generated), **m**aintained (e.g., pride preserved), or **e**nhanced (e.g., joy increased to elation). We use the acronym **PRIME** to describe these emotion regulation goals. Children who regulate emotions well are able to genuinely feel the full range of pleasant and unpleasant emotions, share those emotions with others, and incorporate coping strategies effectively when faced with life's challenges.[3] Children who self-regulate optimally use emotions as cues for how to act and manage behavior in relationships and in school, fostering social and academic competence.[11,19]

Why is Emotional Literacy Important?

Abundant evidence indicates that the emotion knowledge and skills represented by RULER are associated with social competence, physical and psychological health, and academic performance. However, because of the variability in personal and environmental characteristics (nature and nurture), all students may not learn emotional literacy at the same rate. Adding a program that teaches emotional literacy to the standard curriculum can increase the likelihood that students become emotionally literate. Figure 1.1 depicts this idea.

Figure 1.1. Model of emotional literacy

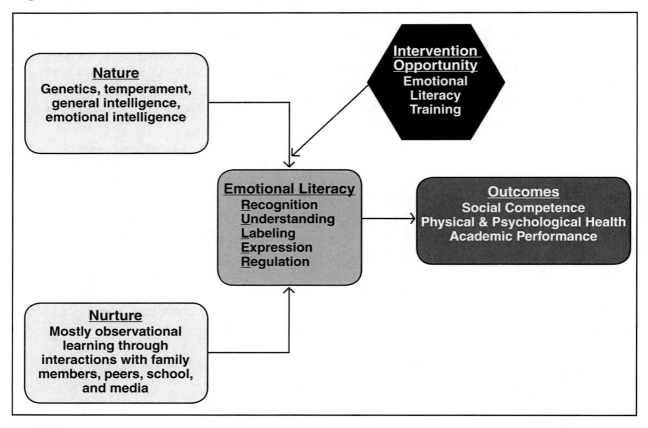

In our model, we propose that the acquisition of emotional literacy is dependent upon two categories of factors: "nature," which students are born with, and "nurture," which students are exposed to during development. The left-hand side of Figure 1.1 depicts these factors. Students may vary in their proclivity to acquire emotion knowledge due in part to their capacity for learning (i.e., general intelligence). Students also may vary in their exposure to emotion knowledge due in part to how they are socialized in their families and classrooms. Incorporating formalized emotional literacy training into school curriculums can minimize the effects of discrepancies in nature and nurture influences. Because emotional literacy is linked to social competence, physical and psychological health, and academic performance, we believe its acquisition is too important to be left to happenstance.

The RULER Approach offers a universal intervention to fill this gap in education. *Emotional Literacy for Students* was designed by psychologists, teachers, administrators, and students to capitalize on the general mission of schools: educating the whole child.[20-23] This program (a) provides developmentally and culturally appropriate instruction for students; (b) helps to create a caring and engaging learning environment; (c) teaches students to apply social and emotional skills both in and outside of school; (d) enhances school performance by addressing the cognitive, emotional, and social dimensions of learning; and (e) encourages school-home partnerships. *Emotional*

Literacy for Students achieves these goals by integrating feeling words through skill-building activities into school curricula in a systematic way.

Preparing for Emotional Literacy for Students

"Communities don't just happen. No teacher, no matter how skilled or well intentioned, can enter a new classroom and announce, 'we are a community.' Communities are built over time, through shared experience, and by providing multiple opportunities for students to know themselves, know one another, and interact in positive and supportive ways."

—M. Sapon-Shevin, Building a Safe Community for Learning[24]

Each student, teacher, classroom, and school is unique. Thus, there is not one "right" way to integrate Emotional Literacy for Students. Teachers who adopt the program participate in workshops and work with a coach to prepare for the program. Teachers acquire strategies that are based on the observations of many teachers who have implemented emotional literacy lessons with great success, as well as on research by educators and psychologists who are experts in preparing schools for integrating SEL programs. In this section, we provide an overview of some of the strategies that teachers adopt when using the program.

From what we have seen in classrooms that use *Emotional Literacy for Students* most effectively, there are four key ways teachers can prepare for the program. Teachers can (1) enhance their own emotional literacy, (2) strengthen relationships with students, (3) hold regular class meetings, and (4) lead open class discussions.

Enhancing Teachers' Emotional Literacy. Teaching *Emotional Literacy for Students* involves being both knowledgeable about emotions and comfortable with myriad emotions—those that are pleasant and those that are unpleasant. The chapters of this book provide an introduction for teachers who want to begin or continue developing skills in order to manage the many different emotions they experience, and that their students and colleagues experience. This chapter, for example, describes briefly the importance of the knowledge that comprises our emotional literacy model and how RULER skills relate to social, emotional, and academic growth. This chapter and Chapter 3 also include information and exercises to enhance emotion skills and to apply these skills in the classroom. By learning about emotional literacy and developing their own RULER skills, educators can make their teaching experiences more enjoyable and their classrooms even more enriching and supportive places for students.

Strengthening Supportive Relationships. Devoting time and energy to building and maintaining strong relationships with students, their families, and others in the school helps teachers develop the support necessary to foster the teaching and learning of emotional literacy. Here we suggest a few ways teachers can strengthen these bonds. Many of these techniques are already a part of skilled teachers' daily practices.

Set clear rules and expectations. Children feel more comfortable and safe when they know what is expected of them. Freed from the anxiety and uncertainty that accompanies a less orderly classroom, students will be emotionally ready to learn.

Use student names. When adults use students' names throughout the school day (e.g., during lessons, passing in the hall, at recess) it helps each student feel valued.

Model and encourage active listening. Active listeners focus their full attention on whoever is speaking, refrain from interrupting, and rephrase what is communicated. Teachers can model active listening by keeping their eyes on students who are talking and responding to them in various ways. For instance, the teacher may paraphrase a student's words or describe the emotions students appear to be feeling with examples of body language, facial expression, or vocal tone. Similarly, teachers can encourage active listening among students by prompting them with questions such as, "What do you think _____ is saying?" or, "How do you think _____ was feeling as he/she told that story?" and, "What makes you think that?" Incorporating active listening into discussions can have a validating effect on students' ideas and feelings. It creates an atmosphere of open communication, enhanced understanding, and increased trust and cooperation. In turn, active listening results in more students sharing their thoughts, opinions, and work.

Demonstrate warmth. A classroom environment in which smiling is commonplace, teachers and students both ask each other how they are and listen for responses, and where all members of the classroom respect each other reduces anxiety related to learning, helps students feel appreciated, increases cooperation, and nurtures prosocial behavior.

Take note of students' feelings. Noticing students' feelings, behavior, and attitudes toward their peers, their teachers, and the school helps teachers to both gauge students' social and emotional skill levels and identify areas for improvement.

Let students learn about their teachers. Students feel more connected to teachers to whom they can relate. Teachers can help their students connect to them by sharing some details of their lives—their childhood, what they liked and disliked about school, or what their current hobbies and interests are. When teachers share about themselves, students will be more comfortable taking risks in sharing their ideas and feelings and are more likely to contribute to classroom discussions and learning.

Respect students' abilities, backgrounds, and varying levels of comfort with receiving positive and negative feedback. Some students thrive on public recognition, but others feel embarrassed when singled out. Teachers should attempt to identify each student's comfort level and communicate praise accordingly. Although it may sometimes be difficult, avoiding public punishment (e.g., yelling at a student in front of the class) is crucial to helping students feel safe and confident in the classroom. Public punishment usually leads to feelings of shame and almost never results in positive behavioral changes.

Curtail inappropriate dialogue. In the rare event that a student becomes inappropriately personal, teachers should conclude the dialogue carefully and address the situation privately with the student, and, if necessary, with the student's parents, the principal, or both.

Enforce rules similarly for all students and let students have a say in setting classroom rules. Students will feel cared for, respected, and empowered when they can make decisions about their learning environment. The Classroom Charter (discussed in the next section) will help to achieve this goal.

Hold Open Class Discussions. A caring environment is fostered when teachers and students to agree upon how everyone in the classroom will communicate with each other, especially during class discussions (including discussions that are explicitly part of Emotional Literacy for Students and those that are not).

Hold Regular Class Meetings. Another way to create a community of learners is to hold daily class meetings. These meetings can be used to both discuss emotions and provide students with opportunities to talk about issues that affect the class. These meetings should be reasonably brief and can take place at any time throughout the day. During morning meetings, for example, teachers can use the Mood Meter (discussed in the next section) to identify the moods and feelings that students (and the teacher) bring to the classroom, and reflect upon how these moods and feelings may influence learning. Meetings held near the end of the school day may be used to create a forum for discussing how students managed their tasks, emotions, and relationships during the school day. Daily meetings can provide a routine structure that supports the development and maintenance of emotional literacy throughout the school day. Meetings allow for celebration of accomplishments, promote reflection and goal setting as a group, and facilitate forgiveness and moving on after difficult events or problems. It is during these class meetings that teachers and students can: make decisions, discuss and solve problems, and set and practice standards for classroom relationships. Meetings also provide opportunities for students to become leaders and facilitators, although the teacher may play this role in initial meetings.

The following suggestions, which have been collected from the field, help make class discussions a positive experience for students and teachers alike.
- Show each other respect by listening attentively and encouraging reinforcement of positive, constructive classroom behavior.
- Allow sufficient time for initial responses from students and then probe for further information if necessary.
- Encourage participation from all students equally. Guard against the temptation to solicit ideas primarily from bright, articulate, and assertive students.
- Encourage non-volunteers. Try to determine why some students tend to remain quiet (i.e., is a particular student shy or does the student have a language disability?). Many students have learned, sometimes painfully, that speaking up in class is unrewarding due to subtle put-downs. Students will not volunteer if they anticipate sarcasm, snide remarks, or hostility in response.

• Prohibit subtle put-down tactics in response to student sharing, regardless of how outlandish a student's point of view may seem or how different it is from what is expected.

Occasionally students will share private experiences and endure ridicule from peers. For example, one teacher reported that a boy disclosed that his worst fear was that he would grow up without any friends, which resulted in a few students making derogatory remarks. In the event that something like this occurs, teachers should turn the discussion around by asking students for suggestions to help with this fear.

Integrating Emotional Literacy into the Classroom

In this section, we describe three anchor tools that are foundational to *Emotional Literacy for Students:* the Classroom Charter, the Mood Meter, and the Blueprint. Then we provide an overview of the Feeling Words Curriculum, which is described more extensively in Chapter 2.

The Anchors

The effectiveness of *Emotional Literacy for Students* is dependent upon the degree to which teachers and students have a basic understanding of emotion-related concepts and experience positive interactions in the classroom. In this section, we highlight three anchor tools that help teachers create a solid foundation for teaching emotional literacy and for enhancing relationships in the classroom. These tools are: the Classroom Charter, the Mood Meter, and the Blueprint. These anchors will help establish classrooms that are interactive communities ideal for implementing *Emotional Literacy for Students.*

Classroom Charter. For a classroom to thrive, all members must share common goals and values that define appropriate behavior.[25] Consider this Classroom Charter written by the fifth grade class in a school in Brooklyn, New York:

> *"We, the 5th graders, believe that our classroom should be a clean, safe, under control, and quiet environment. We need a peaceful environment so that we can learn and grow together in our class. To make this happen, we should be attentive, honest, and trustworthy. We will share our ideas, thoughts, and feelings, and solve problems without hurting each other. We will care for one another and treat each other with respect. Together, we will create a great learning environment for everyone."*

A good first step in creating a caring and responsible classroom community is to start the school year by creating a Classroom Charter. In schools that adopt our program, students are asked how they would like to feel during interactions with their teachers and classmates and what emotions they think are important for success in school. This might begin with a discussion about the different emotions students and teachers experience during class and may include topics relating to the idea that all people have emotions that are valid and worthy of respect. In order for students to be comfortable and open to sharing their feelings, they must trust that their classmates will not use these feelings to tease or hurt them.

We suggest that teachers share how they would like to feel during class activities and interactions and then model positive behavior. Once teachers set the tone, students are encouraged to share their own ideas about the emotions and classroom culture they would like to create, as well as discuss what is important to them. Here is an example of what one teacher said about how she wants to feel:

> "I would like to feel safe and calm in our classroom. I would like this to be a place where we can trust each other and help each other grow. How would each of you like to feel in our classroom? What is most important to you about our classroom?"

This teacher then provided some guidelines for behavior in the classroom:

> "Because we might not want people outside of the class to know some of the information that we will share with each other, it is important that we respect each other and remember that private information is not shared with students or teachers in different classrooms. Throughout the year, you will be encouraged to share your feelings and thoughts, but if you think it might hurt someone else, please keep it to yourself. As a class, we will not tolerate making fun of how another student feels or thinks. Please treat others as you would like to be treated."

This initial discussion opens the door for the development of the Classroom Charter—a vision that everyone in the classroom shares. Students work collaboratively with the teacher to create the Classroom Charter. Classroom Charters we have seen include some of these components:

- Caring for one another
- Treating each other with respect
- Solving problems without hurting each other
- Appreciating each others' differences
- Being honest and trustworthy
- Giving the best effort

Ultimately, the Classroom Charter should establish a positive tone that helps students manage their emotions, relationships, and work routines. Students and their teacher sign the Charter and display it prominently in the classroom. Reciting the Charter should become part of the classroom routine. Some schools choose to combine individual classroom charters into a school-wide charter.

Mood Meter. Identifying and discussing how members of the classroom community—students and teachers—are feeling is at the core of developing emotional literacy. It is also an effective way to start or conclude the school day, lessons, and class meetings. The Mood Meter is a tool designed to help teachers and students become more aware of what they are feeling and how emotions influence thinking, motivation, and behavior. The Mood Meter is a simple graph the represents two components of emotions: feelings and energy (see Figure 1.2 below). The x-axis represents feelings, ranging from unpleasant to pleasant, and the y-axis represents energy level, ranging from low to high. Students and teachers first consider how unpleasant or pleasant they feel and choose the number on the x-axis that best represents their level of pleasantness from -5 (extremely unpleasant) to +5 (extremely pleasant). Next, students and teachers consider how much energy they have and choose the number on the y-axis that best represents their energy level from -5 (no energy at all) to +5 (extremely high energy). Then, students and teachers plot the two numbers (feeling and energy) using an "x" on the graph. They may place their names or the feeling word that corresponds to their current feeling state.

Figure 1.2. The Mood Meter

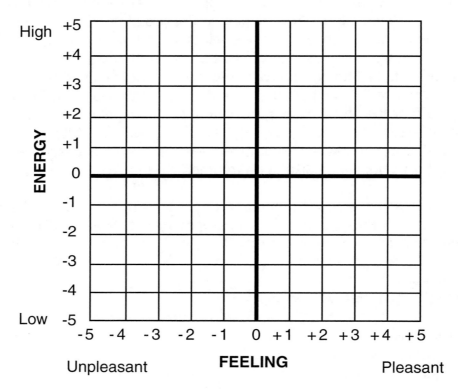

After students plot where they are on the Mood Meter, teachers can encourage them to apply their RULER skills in classroom discussions by posing questions such as:
- What has happened today to make you feel the way you do?
- How did the situation make you feel?
- What kinds of things have you done to express how you have been feeling?
- Have you done anything to change how you have felt?
- How do you feel now?
- Is there anything you could have done or could do to change the way you felt then or feel now?

When teachers introduce the Mood Meter for the first time, they also inform their students that this tool and the discussion questions relate to emotional literacy, a topic that the class will be working on to help students build better relationships with their friends, siblings, and parents. Students are usually quite capable of brainstorming ideas for what they can learn about themselves and others using the Mood Meter. The Mood Meter can be used for individual student learning, whole-class discussions, and as a professional development tool for teachers.

After students are familiar with how the Mood Meter works, teachers and students begin to identify the reasons why a particular quadrant (e.g., low energy/pleasant versus high energy/unpleasant) best describes their present mood. Teachers also regularly use the Mood Meter at the end of a lesson or a school day to find out how students feel about what they learned over the course of the day. If students leave school in the yellow quadrant, with pleasant feelings and high energy, teachers can feel confident that the day's lessons went well. If many students report feeling tired and somewhat negative at the end of the day, the information may have been too difficult, the lesson may not have been explained well, or it just may have been a boring class. The ultimate goal is for teachers and students to build greater emotional self-awareness and feel comfortable sharing their feelings and discussing the activities, situations, and interactions that cause them to feel the way they do.

The Emotional Literacy Blueprint. Creating both an optimal learning environment and a close classroom community makes it more likely that students will be productive, effective, caring, and receptive learners. However, it would be unrealistic to believe that all students will behave appropriately all of the time. Rather than expect or even hope for a classroom without conflict or emotionally charged situations, we suggest having effective strategies on hand for dealing with problems as they arise. Optimal problem solving is the key to managing a classroom effectively and maintaining a culture that enhances emotional literacy and learning in general.

The Emotional Literacy Blueprint is derived from the RULER model[1] and helps students and teachers effectively problem solve about emotional situations. Most situations that cause problems involve emotions; thus the Blueprint is a well-used tool in schools. The Blueprint integrates scientific theory and practical applications to enhance classroom culture while guiding students through a problem-solving method. It can be applied to most emotionally charged incidents, including bullying, failures of personal responsibility (e.g., not completing homework), and other challenges students face. It also can be used to help students plan for upcoming events (e.g., how to face a friend with whom the student has had a fight or how to manage the anxiety associated with taking an important exam). Figure 1.3 presents the basic Blueprint questions and Figure 1.4 shows a more advanced Blueprint, which requires students to problem solve about their own and another person's feelings. Students may write out their responses to the Blueprint questions, or the teacher may walk students through the questions and have them answer the questions aloud.

Figure 1.3. The Blueprint (Beginner)

Question	Student Response
What happened?	
How did I feel?	
What caused me to feel this way?	
How did I express and regulate my feelings?	
What could I have done better?	

Figure 1.4. The Blueprint (Advanced)

What happened? Describe the situation.		
RULER Skill	**Me**	**Other Person**
Recognize and Label	What was I feeling?	What was _____ feeling?
Understand	What caused me to feel this way?	What caused _____ to feel this way?
Express and Regulate	How did I express and regulate my feelings?	How did _____ express and regulate his/her feelings?
Reflect: What could I have done to handle the situation better? How would I have liked the situation to turn out? What can I do now?		

The purpose of the Blueprint is to modify maladaptive behavior, diffuse difficult situations, and prevent those situations from occurring in the first place while at the same time developing students' RULER skills. The Blueprint also facilitates emotional understanding and the awareness of why and how emotions and behavior may need to change in order to maintain an optimal environment for learning. The following anecdote is an example of using the Blueprint to diffuse an emotionally charged situation between two children:

> John and Maria are talking loudly during class. When the teacher asks why they are talking, Maria says she is telling John to stop teasing her and kicking the back of her desk. John stops until the children go out for recess, where he continues to tease Maria. As Maria becomes increasingly upset and attempts to avoid John by moving to a different area to play, John follows her and teases her until she starts to cry. Maria is crying when they come back into the classroom from recess.

Under typical circumstances, the teacher may pull John and Maria aside and ask John to apologize. John is happy to apologize because it allays his guilt and ends the situation. The teacher is happy with the apology because she assumes it has made

John think about what he has done wrong while making Maria feel better. However, there is no lasting effect of the apology. It is likely that John will tease Maria and others again because he has not internalized the impact of his actions on both his own and Maria's emotional states. Using the Blueprint for this situation may help to modify John's behavior in the long term. The following demonstrates one way the Blueprint could be used.

"What happened?" the teacher asks John. John responds that he was trying to get Maria to tell him something. Because John's response does not explain the situation entirely, the teacher guides him to a more detailed description, "What else happened? I think I saw you teasing Maria and kicking her chair."

John says that when Maria would not tell him what he wanted, he began to tease her. The teacher follows up by asking, "How did you feel when you were teasing her?" to push John to recognize and label his feelings. "Angry," John responds.

The teacher then asks him to consider Maria's feelings by recognizing and labeling them, "How do you think Maria felt?" John replies that she probably felt irritated and then embarrassed.

The teacher then helps John begin to understand his feelings and Maria's, "What caused you to feel angry?" He says he was angry because Maria wouldn't answer him. The teacher then asks, "What do you think made Maria irritated and then embarrassed?" John replies that he did not stop bothering her and then she cried in front of the class.

Next, the teacher asks John, "How did you express your anger, and what did you do to handle it?" John replies that he kept bothering Maria. Then, the teacher asks how Maria expressed her irritation. John says she asked him to stop and then cried.

Then, the teacher helps John think about how he will handle similar situations in the future by generating alternative responses for the current one. She asks him, "What could you have done differently to handle the situation better?" John says he could have stopped bothering Maria and waited to see if she would tell him what he wanted to know later.

The teacher offers some additional strategies by suggesting that John also could have tried to understand that Maria may have a good reason for not wanting to tell him and that he could have simply stopped asking.

Finally, the teacher asks if there is anything John can do now to improve the situation with Maria. Having thought about the problem from both his perspective and Maria's, John is able to identify an effective solution to the situation. John tells his teacher that he wants to apologize to Maria and tell her it is okay if she does not want to tell him what he wanted to know.

As this anecdote shows, the Blueprint helps students to resolve conflicts and solve problems, and it helps them develop a greater understanding of themselves and others. The Blueprint can be used for any argument, conflict, or emotionally charged situation students encounter. Schools adopting The RULER Approach integrate the Blueprint into their problem-solving and conflict resolution policies. The Blueprint is often used to help students: (1) identify and understand their feelings; (2) manage their behavior during and after disruptive incidents, and (3) prepare for future events that may cause unwanted emotions, such as anxiety about an upcoming test. The Blueprint questions can be applied to almost any situation and appear throughout the Feeling Words Curriculum as a critical thinking tool for analyzing events from history and characters in literature.

The Feeling Words Curriculum is comprised of units that each focus on one feeling word. Each unit is comprised of a comprehensive set of lessons or "Steps" that provide students with the opportunity to acquire new knowledge and practice their RULER skills—recognizing, understanding, labeling, expressing, and regulating emotion. Each Step helps to create a holistic understanding of RULER skills, dramatically increasing the probability that students store and use the emotion knowledge imparted in the curriculum. Through the Steps, feeling words become whole concepts, with many implications, which ultimately help students govern their lives.

The Feeling Words Curriculum meets the developmental needs of students from kindergarten through eighth grade. The pedagogical techniques and learning tools vary between classrooms for young students (kindergarten through second grades), upper elementary students (third through fifth grades), and middle school students (sixth through eighth grades), however the key elements of the program remain intact. This section provides an overview of the Feeling Words Curriculum, and uses the upper elementary program to illustrate the teaching strategies and learning objectives. First, we define the concept of feeling words as it is used in The RULER Approach and present an overview of the Steps of the Feeling Word Units. Chapter 2 provides a more extensive description of each Step. The Steps are designed to build off of each other; thus, prior to reading about each Step individually it is important to understand the overall approach that is described in this chapter.

What are Feeling Words?

How often do students need to say something but cannot find the right words? This is particularly evident when students want to express their likes and dislikes, feelings, and complex emotional experiences. When the right words are not available, there is a breakdown in communication. Students' thoughts and feelings become confused, remain unexpressed, and in the worst cases, become suppressed or displaced onto others. Unexpressed feelings may result in acting out verbally or physically.

In general, children like to talk about almost everything they experience. Words help them voice their thoughts and feelings, ask for information, and get the attention and affection necessary for optimal development. The need to connect with others underlies efforts to communicate. If connections to others are not realized, children may become alienated, argumentative, depressed, or aggressive. Moreover, when children misidentify their own emotions or those of others, they are likely to generate maladaptive solutions to problems, regardless of their intellectual capacity.

Words play a significant role in the development of children's understanding of emotions.[26-28] In the English language there are thousands of words to describe emotional experiences,[29] yet even most adults have difficulty discussing their emotions with others.[11,30] *Emotional Literacy for Students* helps children learn and use a multitude of words to describe the range of emotions they experience and observe in others. We call this a *feelings vocabulary.* A sophisticated feelings vocabulary contributes to the development of emotional literacy and helps students become aware of their own and others' emotions, communicate emotions effectively, understand the causes and consequences of their emotions, and enhance their ability to regulate emotions and their behavior.[31,32] Connecting words to feelings may even benefit brain development.[33,34]

Children need a wide range of words to communicate effectively. The Feeling Words Curriculum includes vocabulary that characterizes the gamut of emotional experiences children experience and observe. We selected the words based on our review of research on basic emotions such as joy and anger, and more complex, self-evaluative emotions such as *shame* and *pride.*[35,36] We also chose words to reflect different levels of cognitive, social, and emotional development typical for students in different grades. We include various intensities of emotions such as *satisfied, relieved, ecstatic, agitated, regret,* and *ashamed,* as well as terms that elicit emotional reactions such as *bullied, accountable,* and *sympathy.* For example, upon being caught breaking a school rule, a young boy who feels *accountable* for his behavior may experience a flood of emotions, such as *shame, embarrassment,* and *regret.*

In addition to words describing the range of human emotions, words describing motivational and relationship states are included for each grade level. Some of these words include: *competent, challenged, committed,* and *tolerant.* These words are relevant to the classroom environment and can help teachers engage students in conversations about how they can optimize their ability to do well in school and initiate and maintain positive relationships. The words also help students consider how to use their feelings and thoughts to focus on tasks and projects. The families of motivational and relationship words were developed based on research showing that students are more likely to be intrinsically motivated to learn when they feel competent in their abilities, in control of their own behavior, and connected to their school, classmates, and teachers.[37,38] These words reflect how students may feel when motivated (or not) and connected (or not), and can help students identify tactics for making others feel a certain way (e.g., being tolerant of others in a group will help make others feel a sense of security and belonging).

The Units and Steps of the Feeling Words Curriculum

In *Emotional Literacy for Students,* feeling words are the vehicle by which students learn to identify and evaluate their own and others' thoughts, feelings, and behavior; understand the emotions of historical figures and literary characters; describe real-life events and problems; discuss and write articulately about personal experiences; and develop strategies to lead productive and purposeful lives. In these ways, a single feeling word is a world.

The structure of the Feeling Words Curriculum creates continuity in learning from kindergarten through eighth grade. In each year of the curriculum, students learn a set of words that are connected across the years by *feeling word families.* The feeling word families include related vocabulary words that increase in complexity with each grade. For example, the *happy* family begins with *joyful* (kindergarten) and *cheerful* (first grade) which later are followed by *relieved* (fourth grade) and *ecstatic* (fifth grade), with other synonyms or related terms for happiness in the intervening and following years. Students typically learn 15 news words per year. Within a grade level, there is no set order for introducing the words. Teachers can choose feelings words that relate to their standard curricula in subject areas such as language arts, social studies, or health. When teaching about civil rights, a teacher may choose to introduce the word *prejudice.* When teaching about Albert Einstein, a teacher may introduce the word *determined.* Table 1.1 contains a sample of feeling words and their families recommended for two grades in the upper elementary program.

Table 1.1. A sample of feeling word families and words for Grades 4-5

Word family	Grade 4	Grade 5
happy	upbeat	relieved
angry	irate	annoyed
proud	humble	conceited
empowerment	assertive	competent
confused	uncertain	indecisive
autonomy	individuality	unique
anxious	overwhelmed	distressed

Teachers typically begin by teaching one feeling word unit every two to three weeks throughout the school year. Each feeling word unit includes a set of lessons or Steps. The Steps work together so that students thoroughly learn the feeling words and practice their RULER skills across a range of emotions and a variety of contexts (school, home, community) and relationships (teachers, peers, family members). The units for younger students (kindergarten through fifth grade) include five Steps, and those for older students include six Steps. In the remainder of this chapter we present a brief overview of the Steps, which are each explained in detail in the next chapter. The examples are from the upper elementary program.

Step 1: The Personal Association. Learning is optimized when students connect new information to prior experiences and existing knowledge. Step 1 leverages this idea to increase the likelihood that students remember and use feeling words. In this Step, students learn feeling words through questions or visual cues that stimulate thinking about the meaning of the feeling word, evoke personal responses from both the teacher and students, and demonstrate how the feeling word "looks" and "feels." For example, when being introduced to the word *sympathy*, the teacher might present students with pictures taken during Hurricane Katrina and ask them to think about what happened to the people affected by the storm, their homes, and their belongings. Then, the teacher may ask students to share how the images made them feel and whether they have had similar feelings about other people or situations in their lives. Only *after* the teacher and students share their thoughts and feelings does the teacher introduce the feeling word *sympathy* and its formal definition (*sympathy* means to feel sadness for someone who is going through a tough time). The teacher presents the learning experience in a way that both connects teachers to their students and activates each student's existing knowledge base.

Step 2: The Academic and Real World Link. All school subjects, including language arts, math, social studies, physical education, and science involve situations that evoke joy, sadness, irritation, fear, and pride, among other emotions. Current events give rise to a similar range of emotions. In Step 2, the teacher uses feeling words to facilitate students' understanding of course materials and current events, as well as their ability to evaluate how people and groups express and regulate emotions. In this Step, students complete a writing assignment in which they link the new feeling word to course content or a current real-world event using the RULER framework. For example, for the word, *sympathy*, students may write a paragraph about how the abolitionists who started the Underground Railroad may have felt about the slaves, including how the abolitionists expressed themselves, and the strategies they used to regulate their emotions and behavior. This activity looks different for younger students; for kindergarten through second grade, Step 2 is predominantly discussion-based or involves simpler writing or drawings to replace the longer writing assignment described here.

Step 3: The School-Home Partnership. Learning how to both share thoughts and feelings and connect with others is vital to healthy maturation. In Step 3, students become teachers as they introduce feeling words to their family members. Students first share the information from the previous Steps, including their personal experiences and how the word relates to what they have learned in class. Then, students interview family members about a time they experienced the feeling. For example, for the word, *sympathy*, students might ask their parents to describe a time when they felt sad because someone else was sad. The goal is for students and family members to discuss the situations and events that caused them to experience the emotion. Students describe in writing the various situations that caused their family members to experience the emotion. Ideally, students and family members learn about each other by sharing many different personal experiences throughout the year. In this Step, students come in contact with a broad spectrum of human experiences.

Step 4: The Creative Connection. Simultaneously engaging in multiple learning styles leads to the most productive intellectual functioning. Step 4 capitalizes on this strategy. Here, students move away from a literal interpretation of emotions and feelings by characterizing feeling words and their relation to school subjects and real-world situations through art and drama. For example, for the word, *sympathy*, students may dramatize people expressing their condolences to someone at a funeral. This active and exciting Step allows students to visualize, interpret, and produce emotion through visual and performing arts. It also cultivates creativity and spontaneous thinking—an important type of learning that often is stifled at an early age.

Step 5: The Strategy-Building Session. In order to develop healthy relationships, make sound decisions, and deal with life's ups and downs, students must be able to express and regulate their emotions effectively. Teachers and parents alike often tell children to relax, settle down, or pay attention, but it is not always obvious to children how to achieve these goals of calming down or focusing attention. Step 5 involves student-driven discussions that revolve around strategies to express and regulate emotions in order to achieve goals. For example, in a lesson on *sympathy*, a teacher may decide to create small groups in which students brainstorm strategies for how to be more *sympathetic* to others. The impetus for the discussion may be a real-world event like Hurricane Katrina, or a book the class is reading. The goal is for students to hear multiple perspectives, develop goals for regulating emotion, and build a repertoire of strategies for responding to a range of emotions. Step 5 helps students feel more comfortable with their own and others' feelings, be open to differences in opinion and experience, have greater empathy, and ultimately be better equipped to handle challenging moments.

Summary

Emotions are a fundamental component of every learning environment. Thus, a structured approach for educating children and adults about emotions is critical to teaching and learning as well as to creating and maintaining a productive and engaging school environment. The RULER Approach to SEL takes educators and students through a systematic process for accumulating knowledge and acquiring skills that lead to academic, social, and personal success. Together, the RULER Anchor Tools and the Feeling Words Curriculum provide schools with the strategies they need to leverage the emotional aspects of the classroom and, in turn, optimize students' social and intellectual growth and healthy development.

References: Chapter 1

1. Brackett, M. A., & Rivers, S. E. (2011). *The missing link: How emotional literacy promotes personal, academic, and social success.* New York: Teachers College Press (forthcoming).

2. Salovey, P., & Mayer, J. D. (1990). Emotional intelligence. *Imagination, Cognition and Personality,* 9(3), 185-211.

3. Mayer, J. D., & Salovey, P. (1997). What is emotional intelligence? In P. Salovey & D. J. Sluyter (Eds.), *Emotional development and emotional intelligence: Educational implications* (pp. 3-34). New York, NY: Basic Books, Inc.

4. Mayer, J. D., Salovey, P., & Caruso, D. R. (2008). Emotional intelligence: New ability or eclectic traits? *American Psychologist,* 63, 503-517.

5. Ekman, P. (2003). *Emotions revealed.* New York: Henry Holt and Company.

6. Eisenberg, N., Fabes, R. A., Guthrie, I. K., & Reiser, M. (2000). Dispositional emotionality and regulation: Their role in predicting quality of social functioning. *Journal of Personality and Social Psychology,* 78, 136-157.

7. Denham, S. A. (1998). *Emotional development in young children.* New York: Guilford Press.

8. Harris, P. L. (2000). Understanding emotion. In M. Lewis & J. M. Haviland (Eds.), *Handbook of Emotions* (Vol. 2). New York: Guilford Press.

9. Nowicki, S., & Duke, M. P. (2001). Nonverbal receptivity: The Diagnostic Analysis of Nonverbal Accuracy (DANVA). In J. A. Hall & F. J. Bernieri (Eds.), *Interpersonal sensitivity: Theory and measurement* (pp. 183-198). Mahwah, NJ: Lawrence Erlbaum Associates, Publishers.

10. Izard, C. E., Fine, S., Mostow, A., Trentacosta, C., & Campbell, J. (2002). Emotion processes in normal and abnormal development and preventive intervention. *Development and Psychopathology,* 14(4), 761-787.

11. Saarni, C. (1999). *The development of emotional competence.* New York: Guilford Press.

12. Denham, S. A., Blair, K. A., DeMulder, E., Levitas, J., Sawyer, K., Auerbach-Major, S., et al. (2003). Preschool emotional competence: Pathway to social competence. *Child Development,* 74, 238-256.

13. Stein, N. L., & Levine, L. J. (1999). The early emergence of emotional understanding and appraisal: Implications for theories of development. In T. Dalgleish & M. J. Power (Eds.), *Handbook of cognition and emotion* (pp. 383-408). New York: Wiley.

14. Greenberg, M. T., Kusche, C. A., & Riggs, N. (2004). The PATHS curriculum: Theory and research on neurocognitive development and school success. In J. E. Zins, R. P. Weissberg, M. C. Wang & H. J. Walberg (Eds.), *Building academic success on social and emotional learning: What does the research say?* (pp. 170-188). New York, NY: Teachers College Press.

15. Izard, C. E., Fine, S., Schultz, D., Mostow, A., Ackerman, B., & Youngstrom, E. (2001). Emotion knowledge as a predictor of social behavior and academic competence in children at risk. *Psychological Science, 12*(1), 18-23.

16. Izard, C. E. (1989). The structure and functions of emotions: Implications for cognition, motivation, and personality. In I. S. Cohen (Ed.), *The G. Stanley Hall lecture series* (Vol. 9, pp. 39-73). Washington, DC: American Psychological Association.

17. Feldman, R. S., Philippot, P., & Custrini, R. J. (1991). Social competence and nonverbal behavior. In R. S. Feldman & B. Rime (Eds.), *Fundamentals of nonverbal behavior* (pp. 329-350). New York: Cambridge University Press.

18. Pennebaker, J. W. (1997). *Opening up: The healing power of expressing emotions.* New York: Guilford Press.

19. Lopes, P. N., & Salovey, P. (2004). Toward a broader education: Social, emotional and practical skills. In J. E. Zins, R. P. Weissberg, M. C. Wang & H. J. Walberg (Eds.), *Building academic success on social and emotional learning: What does the research say?* (pp. 76-93). New York, NY: Teachers College Press.

20. Shriver, T. P., & Weissberg, R. P. (2005, August 16). No emotion left behind. *New York Times.*

21. Zins, J. E., Weissberg, R. P., Wang, M. C., & Walberg, H. J. (Eds.). (2004). *Building academic success on social and emotional learning: What does the research say?* New York: Teachers College Press.

22. Raver, C. C., & Zigler, E. F. (1991). Three steps forward, two steps back: Head Start and the measurement of social competence. *Young Children, 46*(4), 3-8.

23. Zigler, E. F., & Bishop-Josef, S. J. (2006). The cognitive child vs. the whole child: Lessons from 40 years of Head Start. In D. G. Singer, R. M. Golinkoff & K. Hirsh-Pasek (Eds.), *Play = learning: How play motivates and enhances children's cognitive and social-emotional growth* (pp. 15-35). New York: Oxford University Press.

24. Sapon-Shevin, M. (1995). Building a safe community for learning. In W. Ayers (Ed.), *To become a teacher: Making a difference in children's lives* (pp. 99-112). New York: Teachers College Press.

25. Johnson, D. W., & Johnson, R. T. (2004). The three Cs of promoting social and emotional learning. In J. E. Zins, R. P. Weissberg, M. C. Wang & H. J. Walberg (Eds.), *Building academic success on social and emotional learning: What does the research say?* (pp. 40-58). New York, NY: Teachers College Press.

26. Russell, J. A. (1990). The preschoolers' understanding of the causes and consequences of emotion. *Child Development, 61,* 1872-1881.

27. Kopp, C. B. (1989). Regulation of distress and negative emotions: A developmental view. *Developmental Psychology, 25*(3), 343-354.

28. Harre, R. (1986). *The social construction of emotions.* Oxford: Basil Blackwell.

29. Averill, J. R. (1980). On the paucity of positive emotions. In K. Blankstein, P. Pliner & J. Polivy (Eds.), *Advances in the study of communication and affect: Vol. 6 Assessment and modification of emotional behavior* (pp. 7-45). New York: Plenum.

30. Zajonc, R. B. (1980). Feeling and thinking: Preferences need no inferences. *American Psychologist,* 35, 161-175.

31. Olson, D. R., Astington, J. W., & Harris, P. L. (1988). Introduction. In J. W. Astington, P. L. Harris & D. R. Olson (Eds.), *Developing theories of mind* (pp. 1-19). Cambridge, England: Cambridge University Press.

32. Hesse, P., & Cicchetti, D. (1982). Perspectives on an integrated theory of emotional development. *New Directions for Child Development,* 16, 3-48.

33. Sylwester, R. (1995). *A celebration of neurons: An educator's guide to the human brain.* Alexandra, VA: Association for Supervision and Curriculum Development.

34. Caine, R., & Caine, G. (1994). *Making connections: Teaching and the human brain.* Menlo Park, CA: Addison-Wesley.

35. Abe, J. A., & Izard, C. E. (1999). The developmental functions of emotions: An analysis in terms of differential emotions theory. *Cognition and Emotion,* 13(5), 523-549.

36. Plutchik, R. (2003). *Emotions and life: Perspectives from psychology, biology, and evolution.* Washington, DC: American Psychological Association.

37. Deci, E. L., & Ryan, R. M. (1985). *Intrinsic motivation and self-determination in human behavior.* New York: Plenum.

38. Deci, E. L., Vallerand, R. J., Pellietier, L. G., & Ryan, R. M. (1991). Motivation and education: The self-determination perspective. *Educational Psychologist,* 26(3 & 4), 325-346.

Chapter 2
The Feeling Words Curriculum

*Marc A. Brackett, Marvin Maurer, Susan E. Rivers, Nicole A. Elbertson,
Janet Pickard Kremenitzer, Bruce E. Alster, Marilyn D. Carpenter,
Laura Stuart-Wonderlie, Patty Cassella, and Jonathon Bauer*

Overview

In the Feeling Words Curriculum, teachers introduce a new feeling word unit, consisting of a set of five Steps, every two to three weeks. The structure of the Feeling Words Curriculum provides students with regular opportunities to develop and practice using their RULER skills while also acquiring a sophisticated vocabulary to describe their own feelings and those of family members and the characters and people they encounter in literature, history, and current events. In this chapter we present the five Steps of the upper elementary curriculum. The Steps for other grade levels are similar but are tailored to the developmental levels and needs of students in lower elementary (kindergarten through second grades) and middle school (sixth through eighth grades) classrooms.

Step 1: The Personal Association

In *Step 1, The Personal Association,* students connect personally to new feeling words. We designed this Step specifically to enhance the understanding, retention, and application of feeling words.

Teaching Step 1

Step 1 consists of two parts: (1) relating the meaning of the feeling word to students' experiences and knowledge, and (2) formally introducing the feeling word.

Relating the meaning of the feeling word to students' experiences and knowledge. In part one of Step 1, teachers introduce a feeling word that corresponds to an upcoming lesson and then pose reflection questions. When teachers introduce the word, they share personal connections to the word—using the meaning of the word but not the word itself—by telling a story from their own lives or by using visual aids such as movie clips, songs, or images. After sharing their experiences, teachers pose a question so that students can reflect on their own experiences. Questions can be asked in a number of ways to encourage student participation. Effective question stems include: Have you ever…? Can you remember…? Who has ever…? When have you…? Can you think of a time when…? Has someone you know…? What kinds of situations make students feel…?

For example, when introducing the word *sympathy*, a teacher may share a story about the time her close friend's dog died. The teacher then asks students to describe how they would feel if their friend lost a pet or a loved one. The teacher also may ask students to think about how other people would feel in the same situation (this is a useful way to frame the question when students are reluctant to talk about themselves). Or, the teacher may show the class an image that evokes or represents the word, such as a person who has been injured.

The technique of the teacher sharing first helps students recall their own experiences related to the feeling word and makes them feel more comfortable sharing with the class. Students often need time to reflect on their own lives and identify a relevant experience. Allowing students to first write out their experience gives them time to gather their thoughts before sharing them aloud. Once students have ample time to identify and reflect on their own experiences, teachers ask for volunteers to share their experiences. Clearly, because of the time involved, not every student can share during every lesson. Teachers can maximize sharing by having students work in pairs or in groups. Even students who do not share an experience benefit by being exposed to the meaning of the word through listening to their classmates' stories, as well as by reflecting on their own experiences.

Most of the time, students are eager to share their experiences. They think of it as a show-and-tell of their life stories. At times, students may provide inappropriate examples or be reluctant to share anecdotes. To achieve the learning objectives of this Step, it is imperative that each student's anecdote answers the initial question completely and accurately. For example, "I was happy yesterday," does not provide sufficient information to demonstrate an understanding of the meaning of the word *ecstatic*. A better response would be, "One time when I was skateboarding, I did a really hard trick on the neighbor's porch, and I felt really happy. It was the first time I did it and didn't fall. It was great!" If a student provides an incomplete response to the question, the teacher can coax the desired response by asking simple questions such as, "How did that make you feel?" or, "Why did you feel that way?" The degree to which students seem to understand the feeling word should determine the number of experiences shared for each word.

To help students generate accurate examples and encourage them to participate, we recommend that teachers share additional personal anecdotes and ask guiding questions as often as possible. Our work in schools indicates that students feel considerably more connected to the classroom when their teachers are open about their own experiences.

Teachers can introduce the meaning of the feeling word at any point in the day—during a morning meeting, reading/story time, or within any lesson. Teachers typically develop a routine for introducing feeling words so students can anticipate the emotional literacy lessons, just as they do other aspects of the curriculum.

Formally introducing the feeling word. After introducing the meaning of the feeling word and asking students to connect its meaning to their own experiences in a short class discussion, the teacher introduces the feeling word and its formal definition. One way the teacher does this is to say:

> "There is a word that describes the experiences we are all sharing. That word is sympathy. The word, *sympathy*, means a feeling of sadness for someone who is going through a tough time."

When teachers define the word, they both say the word and write out the word and its definition. To reinforce learning, students repeat the word and its definition aloud, and also write the feeling word and its definition on a "graphic organizer" or in an emotional literacy journal. See Figure 2.1 for a sample of student writing for the word *frightened*.

Figure 2.1. Student writing sample: Step 1, for the word *frightened*

My experience: I was afraid the other night when the electricity went out in our house. It was really dark, and I couldn't see anything. We couldn't find any flashlights, which made me even more scared.

Feeling word: frightened

Definition: afraid of or fearful about something

We encourage teachers to use new feeling words often in their interactions with students. We also recommend designating a place in the classroom to be used as "The Feeling Word Wall," where each feeling word can be added once it is introduced.

Table 2.1 presents a summary of Step 1.

Table 2.1. Summary of Step 1

1. The teacher selects a feeling word that corresponds with an upcoming lesson in another content area.
2. The teacher shares a personal experience, incorporating a demonstration of the word's meaning through a visual aid or music when useful.
3. Students write about and then share their personal experiences connected to the meaning of the word.
4. The teacher formally introduces the feeling word and its definition.
5. Students write out the word and its definition and use the new feeling word in a written description of their experience.

Pedagogical Significance of Step 1

The techniques used in this Step involve students actively engaging in the learning process and help them to make personal connections with the feeling word. Students are not sitting passively at their desks attempting the rote task of memorizing a definition. Instead, they are engaged in thinking about how the word "feels" and "looks" before the teacher presents the actual word and its meaning. This helps students connect the feeling word to their prior knowledge – knowledge that is based on their intellectual, personal, and emotional experiences. When students connect the new word to existing knowledge, teachers sustain students' curiosity and attention. As a result, students are more likely to enjoy learning, to process social information and academic material with greater ease, and to problem solve more effectively.

Another benefit of the techniques used in Step 1 is that they help students understand that both their teachers and classmates have had experiences similar to their own. All members of the classroom community have the opportunity to share experiences and anecdotes with each other, which helps create a caring classroom where students feel valued and safe to share personal experiences. At the same time, it exposes students to multiple perspectives. Students usually feel more connected to their classmates and teachers when they realize others have had experiences similar to their own. Realizing that others have had different life experiences helps students to develop empathy (i.e., understanding events from someone else's point of view).

Learning Objectives of Step 1

In Step 1, students acquire and use new vocabulary to describe emotional experiences. Students are developing their RULER skills. They are learning how to:
- **Recognize** feelings in themselves by connecting vocabulary words to personal experiences (e.g., how *sympathy* feels and looks);
- **Understand** what events cause these feelings to occur (e.g., what causes people to feel *sympathy*);
- **Label** emotions properly in order to be more effective communicators (e.g., *sympathy* as opposed to sadness is the best word to describe the feelings we have for someone who has lost a loved one); and
- **Express** or share feelings with others (e.g., feel comfortable discussing what makes us feel sympathy; learn that it is natural to feel *sympathy*).

Acquiring this knowledge and practicing these skills helps students develop and use effective strategies that prepare them to regulate their emotions.

The pedagogical approach in this Step also helps students develop interpersonal skills such as active listening and empathy. Teachers encourage students to ask each other follow-up questions and to acknowledge each other's experiences in positive ways (e.g., smiles, nods).

Step 2: The Academic and Real World Link

In **Step 2, The Academic and Real World Link,** students make explicit links between new feeling words and the standard academic curricula in one or more content areas, such as language arts, social studies, science, math, health, civics, or current events.

Teaching Step 2

Either for homework or class assignments, students perform a character analysis using the new feeling word along with the RULER framework. Teachers typically select a story, novel, or real-world event in the newspaper for students to work from, or they allow students to choose their own content to analyze. Students either read the article aloud, together with the class, or individually to themselves. Then they conduct the character analysis. In their analysis, students:
- Examine how the characters, historical figures, or people in the real world feel, taking into consideration their particular place in history or their specific situation;
- Identify and describe how one or more characters or individuals experienced the feeling word; and
- Provide specific evidence to support their opinions, observations, and connections.

Teachers use the RULER framework to guide student discussions. Some questions for each area of RULER include:

<u>R</u>ecognize
- What was the character feeling?
- What clues did you use to make this judgment?

<u>U</u>nderstand
- What caused the character to feel that particular way?
- Can you understand why the character felt this way?
- Would you have felt similarly or differently? Why?

<u>L</u>abel
- What other emotions were present (besides the assigned feeling word)?

<u>E</u>xpress
- How did the character express these emotions?
- How did others respond to this emotional expression?
- Was this the best way to express these emotions (i.e., Was anyone offended? Did others understand what the character was feeling?)?
- Could the character have expressed these emotions more effectively?

<u>R</u>egulate
- What did the character do to handle these emotions?
- In what ways was this effective? In what ways was this ineffective?
- What could the character have done differently to manage these emotions?
- What could other characters in the story have done to help the character regulate his/her emotions?

The character analysis may be done in large or small group discussions, in writing, or a combination of the two. Once students gain experience doing character analyses, they benefit the most from conducting a written analysis and then discussing their ideas with others in small groups or with the whole class.

Figure 2.2 shows an example of a fifth grader's character analysis using the word sympathy.

Figure 2.2. Step 2: Character Analysis for the Word Sympathy

Name of person, group or character:
Kevin

What was the person or group feeling?
Kevin felt sympathy for Max.

What do you think caused these feelings?
Kevin felt sympathy for Max because he knew Max was going through tough times. Max is sick a lot and does not do well in school. Max also doesn't have friends.

How were these feelings expressed and handled?
Kevin and Max became close friends. Kevin taught Max how to read and how to use his imagination, showing Max that he really cared about him. Kevin also helped Max a lot in school. Eventually he was feeling better and was even able to join the honors class.

Did this work well? What else could have worked?
I think Kevin did a great job at helping Max. Maybe he could have talked to more children in school so they wouldn't have made fun of Max.

Virtually every book and story involves characters who experience emotions. Thus, it should not be difficult for teachers to find a plethora of examples for conducting character analyses using the feeling words and RULER framework.

Table 2.2 provides a summary of Step 2.

Table 2.2. Summary of Step 2

1. The teacher selects content (newspaper article or book) or allows students to select content from which to choose a character and perform a character analysis.

2. Students work in groups or individually to analyze the character using a set of questions guided by the RULER framework.

3. Students describe their character analysis in writing.

4. Students discuss their character analyses with the class.

Pedagogical Significance of Step 2

Step 2 provides opportunities for students to integrate new vocabulary into their everyday conversations and experiences. It also enriches student learning by connecting academic materials to cognitive, social, and emotional processes. Linking feeling words to other lessons and real-world events helps students understand new words in terms of the individuals and characters both in the content area and in the world in which they live.

In Step 2, students learn how to observe and articulate the role emotions play in the actions and thoughts of characters they encounter in literature, history, the real world, and other subject areas. All lessons in literature, social studies, and current events invariably involve people who experience the gamut of emotions – relief, self-doubt, irritation, disappointment, satisfaction, and so forth. Learning about feelings in the context of academic materials and real-world events powerfully illustrates that emotions are central to all aspects of life. It also helps students develop compassion and empathy, which are foundational to healthy development. When studying the war in Iraq, for example, students can write about and discuss the traumatic experiences of soldiers and the impact of war on the soldiers' lives. In poetry classes, students can analyze the causes and consequences of a particular character's excessive love for someone. In science, students can discuss the feelings of scientists who make discoveries as well as the implications of the discoveries to people and the world.

Finally, when students peruse magazine and newspaper articles with the goal of linking feeling words to a particular topic, they are simultaneously developing emotional literacy skills while learning about how emotions are interwoven in all aspects of daily life. The more students connect what they learn in school to everyday life (and connect what they observe in everyday life to learning), the greater the probability they will be good communicators, informed citizens, critical thinkers, and successful problem solvers. The more students analyze and write about subjects taught in school, the more likely they will learn the material and succeed in school.

Learning Objectives of Step 2

In this Step, students use feeling words and the RULER framework to describe characters in literature, history, and real-world events. In their writing and in class discussions, students should demonstrate skills in:
- **Recognizing** emotion by identifying the emotions of characters (e.g., describe the clues which demonstrate that a character in a story is experiencing a particular emotion);
- **Understanding** emotions by describing the causes and potential consequences or benefits of emotions;
- **Labeling** emotions by applying new vocabulary to the emotions expressed by characters;
- **Expressing** emotions by discussing the ways characters express their emotions; and
- **Regulating** emotions by describing the effective and ineffective strategies characters use to handle their emotions.

Through this process, students develop reading comprehension, writing, and critical thinking skills. These skills are enhanced as students:

- Look for facts and details to connect the subject matter with the feeling word;
- Identify the intentions of an author when a character is presented in a particular way;
- Examine sequences of emotion-laden events to draw conclusions about why the events occurred in a particular way;
- Make predictions about how different events affect the emotions of historical figures or characters in a story;
- Make inferences based on the emotions of characters and events;
- Compare and contrast the emotions of characters to determine their relationships with each other; and
- Interpret the use and impact of figurative language.

Step 3: School-Home Partnership

Step 3, the School-Home Partnership, promotes active family involvement in learning. In this Step, students become teachers as they introduce feeling words to members of their family and other important adults in their lives. Students also deepen their comprehension of feeling words and learn more about the lives of their family members and other important adults.

Teaching Step 3

Step 3 brings classroom learning home. For this Step, students discuss a feeling word with an important adult in their lives, usually a family member. Based on their work from Steps 1 and 2, students share personal experiences relevant to the feeling word and consider how the word relates to material they learned in class (i.e., course materials, current events). For example, for the word *selfish*, a student may say:

> "Mom, I just learned the word *selfish*; it means to take care of oneself without thinking of others. I shared with my class a time when I was really selfish. Remember when I told Ryan I didn't want him to come with us to the movies? He was really upset, but I just wanted to be with you by myself. I know that I was being *selfish* because I didn't want him there. I feel bad that I made him upset. Then, in social studies, we learned about this leader who was really *selfish*. He wanted all the money and armies for himself and didn't want to share them with the leader from another country. I wrote about how this person was thinking only about himself and didn't care that the other country needed help. Just like I was only thinking about what I wanted and didn't care about how that made Ryan feel."

After introducing the feeling word to a family member, students ask that person about a time when he or she experienced the feeling. Here is an example of a discussion between a boy and his grandmother about the word eager:

> Boy
> "Grandma, the new feeling word I learned at school today was *eager*. It means to feel excited for something and ready for it to

happen. I was *eager* to start basketball practice last month. I had to wait six months until it was the right season. In school, we learned about Lewis and Clark's expedition. They were *eager* to return to St. Louis after spending over two years on the expedition. As they approached St. Louis on their boat, they saw thousands of people gathered along the shore to greet them. Those people also must have been *eager* for their return. Can you tell me about a time when you were *eager*—excited for something and ready for it to happen?"

Grandmother
"I was *eager* for you to be born. You were my first grandchild, and I just could not wait for your mom to give birth to you. I had the biggest smile on my face when I told my friends I was going to be a grandma."

Students then write a paragraph detailing their conversations. The paragraph can describe the family member's experience and the causes or consequences of the feeling. Teachers evaluate student writing based on the extent to which it demonstrates an accurate understanding of the feeling word.

Teachers may vary the level of specificity required in the written portion of the assignment to address the needs of their students and to keep the task interesting and challenging. They may also provide additional instructions to students helping order to guide the discussions. Teachers may encourage students to interview several family members or adults, which will provide them with more exposure to other people's experiences with the same feeling. Or they may ask students to explore:
- The similarities and differences between their own experiences and those of their family members;
- The causes of the feelings; and
- How the feelings were expressed and handled:
  — Did you want to feel more or less of this emotion?
  — Did you express this emotion in a way that was helpful or hurtful to others and to yourself?

Students who are doing this Step for the first time may do mock interviews in the classroom, guided by the teacher, to practice asking questions and recording details of stories in writing.

When students return to the classroom with their written assignments, teachers guide them in a class discussion in which they share what they have learned. Teachers help students compare and contrast their own experiences with the different experiences of adults. For example, in one classroom, a teacher drew a Venn diagram to illustrate the similarities and differences in the causes of annoyance in students and their family members, as shown in Figure 2.3. Teachers also model for students how to listen attentively as members of the class share stories. They encourage students to demonstrate that they are paying attention to each other by nodding their heads, smiling, and providing other nonverbal and verbal affirmations, such as asking questions that incorporate details of the story. Table 2.3 provides a summary of Step 3.

Figure 2.3. "Things That Make Us Annoyed."

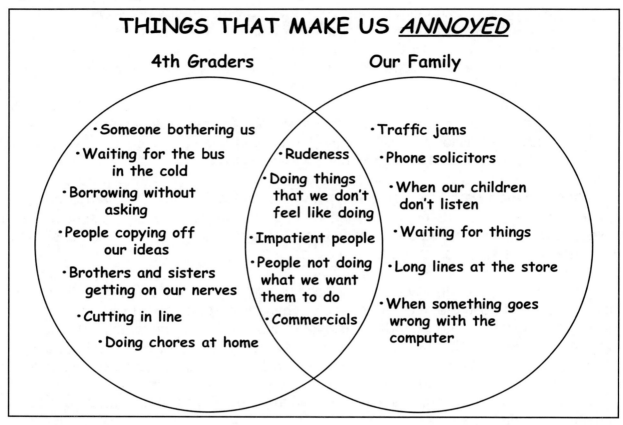

Table 2.3. Summary of Step 3

---

1. For homework, students teach an adult family member the feeling word and share what they have learned about the word.

2. Students interview the adult family member about his/her experience with the word.

3. Students describe in writing the adult family member's experience.

4. In class, students may share and discuss the experiences about which they learned.

Pedagogical Significance of Step 3

The pedagogical significance of Step 3 is twofold. First, Step 3 involves parents in the learning process, which contributes to enriching and successful learning experiences for students. Parents who are actively engaged in their children's learning follow their development, reinforce the expectations of the schools, and monitor their children's well-being and learning. In fact, parental involvement in education is an integral part of the *No Child Left Behind Act* of 2001, which advocates that schools encourage parental involvement to promote the social, emotional, and academic growth of children.

Second, Step 3 provides students the opportunity to use feeling words in contexts outside of the classroom and to connect feeling words to the experiences of other important people in their lives. In doing so, students develop a deeper understanding of their own and others' feelings. When students hear about and describe in writing the emotional experiences of family members, they come in personal contact with a wide range of human emotions to which they ordinarily would not be exposed. When students connect their own experiences to those of their family members, they also gain insight into the significance of their own feelings and those of others.

There are many benefits of the pedagogical approach of Step 3 to teachers, students, and their families. Some of the benefits we have seen in our work in schools as well as documented in scientific literature include the following:
- Students and their family members learn about each others' feelings and the importance of emotions in daily life. This process promotes family compatibility and personal growth, and also prepares students to integrate successfully into mainstream society.
- Family members become more familiar with what their children are learning across the curriculum, not just in emotional literacy lessons.
- When students discuss their personal feelings and experiences with family members, many of their basic psychological needs are attended to—trust, sense of belonging, and sense of purpose. When these needs are met, students are more likely to attain higher levels of intellectual, emotional, and social skills.[1]
- Family members and students assume the role of both student and teacher, which creates an ideal environment for learning. Students also gain a sense of ownership by being in control of their learning experiences.
- By being actively engaged in their child's learning through regular discussions, parents will be more likely to perceive the school as a warm, welcoming place to which they can contribute. They also will develop positive associations with students' learning and will continue to be involved.

Learning Objectives of Step 3

In Step 3, students learn about their family members by sharing personal experiences, which provides them with exposure to a broad spectrum of human experiences as well as the opportunity to talk about the causes and consequences of emotions and ways to handle different emotions. This process helps students to develop their RULER skills by
- **Recognizing** how others experience different emotions;
- **Understanding** what causes those emotions and their consequences;
- **Labeling** emotions using new vocabulary;
- **Expressing** their emotions with others in socially appropriate ways (through sharing stories); and
- Discussing effective and ineffective strategies for **regulating** emotions.

Students also learn about themselves during the process of learning about other people, which fosters self-awareness and empathy. Students practice their oral and written communication skills in this Step, as well as their active listening skills. Students have multiple opportunities to use the new feeling word as they teach it to their family members, write about their experiences, and describe those experiences in class discussions; these activities deepen and broaden learning.

Step 4: The Creative Connection

In *Step 4, The Creative Connection,* students move away from a literal interpretation of emotions and use the visual and performing arts to express emotions.

Teaching Step 4

In this Step, students design symbols or scenes (visual arts) or create a tableau or theatrical presentation (performing arts) to represent feeling words. They present their creation to their classmates and articulate how the image or performance represents the feeling word. Teachers then guide students in a discussion to encourage deeper thinking and analysis about how the creation represents the feeling word.

The following is an overview of how students use the visual and performing arts to represent feeling words.

Visual arts. Working individually or in small groups, students create a representation of the feeling word using symbols or scenes. They use colors, lines, shapes, and textures to characterize the feeling word (e.g., glue and sand for a rough surface to represent *uneasy*). Students also may choose images from magazines, newspapers, or the internet to characterize the feeling word. Younger students use more simple, concrete representations. For example, a third grade student symbolized the word *puzzled* through his computer-made design of a face with an open mouth surrounded by question marks (see Figure 2.4). Another student represented the word *excluded* using a cartoon from a magazine (see Figure 2.5). Scenes may depict real world events (e.g., incidents that occur on the playground, in the school cafeteria, at a sports game, on a television program or commercial) or events related to a topic in other content areas (e.g., language arts, science, social studies, character education). With experience, student drawings progress from symbols to more complex and abstract scenes, including paintings, storyboards, cartoon strips, or collages. After creating the symbol or scene, students write a few sentences explaining how it represents the feeling word, and then share their work during classroom discussions. In their writing and oral presentations, students are required to articulate the reasons why their symbol or scene represents the feeling word, specifying which details from their creation support their argument.

Figure 2.4. Symbol for the word 'puzzled'

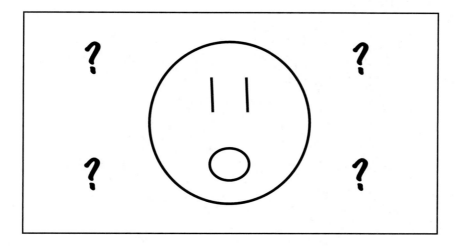

Figure 2.5. Scene for the word 'excluded'

Some examples of students' writing that describes how the scene represents the feeling word follow.

In one fifth grade classroom, a teacher asked students to relate the feeling word, *optimistic*, to a television commercial. As shown in Figure 2.6, one student drew a scene from a shampoo commercial and wrote a short explanation how specific elements in the commercial represented the term, *optimistic*. This student artist wrote that the commercial tried to make people feel like this particular shampoo would make them look the best they possibly could.

Figure 2.6. Scene for the word 'optimistic': Pantene makes you feel optimistic and your hair shine like the sun!

For the word *enraged*, a group of fourth grade students drew a scene from the Boston Tea Party (Figure 2.7). These students explained that King George was *enraged* when the colonists refused to pay taxes on the tea and revolted against the King. In their scene, they showed the colonists who were dressed up as the Mohawk Indians, throwing tea into the Boston Harbor.

Figure 2.7. Scene for the word 'enraged': The Boston Tea Party

Performing arts. Working in small groups, students use the performing arts to create a dramatic representation of the feeling word. Dramatic representations may take the form of a tableau or a short theatrical presentation. A tableau is a "frozen moment." Using their bodies, students illustrate the meaning of the feeling word in a quick, freeze frame. A short theatrical performance or skit is more elaborate than the tableau because it includes a beginning (to set the time and location of the story), a middle (to demonstrate a rising action; i.e., the "issue" with which the characters have to deal or cope), and an end (to show the climax of the story and how the characters resolve the issue). In their performing arts creation, students may represent the feeling word using real world events, such as a birthday party or bullying situation, or relate the word to content covered in a subject area, such as social studies or literature.

In one classroom, the teacher gave students three minutes to create a tableau representing the word bullied. One group of students designed a tableau showing a group of students picking on a girl (see Figure 2.8). Another group of students created a scene in which they hurt one boy's feelings, first by making fun of him and then by not allowing him to play a game.

Figure 2.8. Tableau for the word 'bullied': "We don't like you!"

When students work in small groups to create the visual or performing arts representation, teachers encourage collaborative efforts. Each student should contribute ideas to the project; listen to others' ideas; work with the group, compromising when necessary, to develop a final project; and actively participate in the creation of the project.

After students perform their tableau or skit, teachers guide discussions using the RULER framework. Teachers ask students to:
- **Recognize** and **label** all the feelings represented in the performance (most performances include many more feelings than just the targeted feeling word);
- **Understand** the causes and consequences of the feelings by
  —Identifying the causes of the feelings represented;
  —Considering the consequences of how the feelings were **expressed** in the depicted scene (were the feelings expressed in ways that were helpful to the various characters or hurtful to them?); and
- Generate strategies for **regulating** (or handling) the feelings and the situation in ways that are helpful to the various characters involved.

In their training on the Feeling Words Curriculum, teachers learn how to guide discussions to help students identify helpful strategies for handling or regulating emotions. For example, if the scene represents more negative experiences, the teacher guides the discussion towards identifying strategies for preventing such situations from occurring and dealing with the feelings that arise from these situations. If the scene represents more positive experiences, the teacher guides the discussion towards developing strategies for fostering pleasant feelings and helpful ways to communicate those feelings to others. Teachers also help students identify ways to sustain or increase the intensity of positive emotions, or restrain positive emotions so that they can be experienced at a more appropriate time and place (e.g., after the teacher finishes teaching a lesson).

Table 2.4 provides a summary of Step 4.

Table 2.4. Summary of Step 4

---

1. Students design symbols or scenes (visual arts) or create a tableau or theatrical presentation (performing arts) to represent the feeling word.

2. Students present their creation to their classmates and explain how the image or performance represents the feeling word.

3. The teacher guides students in a discussion to encourage deeper thinking and analysis about how the creation represents the feeling word.

Pedagogical Significance of Step 4

Step 4 offers a valuable experiential learning technique for teachers to introduce into their classrooms. This active and engaging Step allows students to visualize, interpret, and produce images on paper and with their bodies. Students think about feelings and academic material in innovative ways, practice generating different feelings to illustrate a dramatic message, and work cooperatively. When students represent a feeling word using the visual and performing arts, they have the opportunity to experience a variety of personae and see story plots from multiple angles. This Step also sustains students' interest and excitement about learning and increases their ability to store and remember information. In this Step, students practice transferring what they are learning in the classroom to both their personal lives and the real world. This process enhances their emotional literacy, knowledge of the subject area, and higher-order thinking skills.

The pedagogical approach used in Step 4 capitalizes on what neuroscientists have recently discovered about the learning process. Generally speaking, the right hemisphere is more involved in visual, nonverbal, spatial, divergent, and intuitive thinking, and the left hemisphere is activated especially by verbal, logical, categorical, detailed-oriented, and convergent thinking and analysis.[2,3] The most productive intellectual functioning occurs when there is joint activation by both sides of the brain. The symbolic representations and dramatic performances that are part of Step 4 require involvement between both hemispheres. The activities that comprise this Step help students utilize mental skills that often are not involved in more traditional, formal instruction techniques such as reading and memorizing information. Research shows that training in various forms of imaginative play, such as those encouraged in Step 4, has significant effects on imagination, creativity, self-control, persistence, adjustment to school, perspective-taking ability, and experiencing positive emotions. It also has a direct impact on academic achievement, including better verbal and math skills.[4-6]

Step 4 encourages creative, nonverbal, and intuitive processing of information— the kind of learning that is often stifled at an early age. Young children, with crayons or make-believe play, create all kinds of artistic representations. In doing so, they are writing and telling stories. Once children reach the upper elementary grades, such play is derided, perceived as trivial or irrelevant to academic learning and achievement.[7] Yet, in order for students to sustain focus, there must be active and fun components in their attempts to understand the world. Step 4 provides those components. Teachers report that this Step offers a valuable experiential learning technique, creating learning opportunities in which students are engaged and active. Teachers and students alike tell us that Step 4 is the most fun to do, watch, and discuss.

Learning Objectives of Step 4

In Step 4, students use visual or performing arts to represent the feeling word. They articulate orally and in writing how the representation depicts the feeling word, referring to specific elements of the design or performance to support their interpretations. Through the process, students learn how to:

- **Recognize** and **label** how emotions are represented in objects, places, and symbols (e.g., a question mark for *puzzled*) and in scenes representing topics in different school subjects or real-world events (e.g., how the Pilgrims may have felt when they disembarked from the Mayflower; how bullies frighten students when teachers are not watching).
- **Understand** that
  —Feelings occur in multiple contexts;
  —Different objects represent feelings for people in unique ways;
  —Feelings are part of myriad real-world events; and
  —"Characters" in social studies, literature, and other subjects experience the same emotions they do.
- **Express** their understanding of emotions in a variety of ways (verbally and with their bodies), and identify the appropriate ways, times, and places to express their emotions.
- Identify strategies to handle or **regulate** feelings and behaviors in real-world settings, both their own feelings and behaviors and those of others.

Step 5: Strategy-Building Session

In **Step 5, The Strategy-Building Session,** students develop the ability to handle or regulate their feelings in ways that are helpful to themselves and others. Students also acquire a repertoire of strategies to both express their feelings in socially acceptable ways and regulate the experience of an emotion.

Teaching Step 5

Overview. In Step 5, students learn how to express and regulate a wide range of emotions. By discussing characters in books, historical figures, and people in everyday life, students identify strategies for expressing and regulating emotions. Teachers may revisit a topic the class discussed as part of Step 1 (*Personal Association*) or Step 2 (*Academic and Real World Link*) to use as a starting point for the strategy-building session. However, it often happens that situations occur among the students or in school that can be serve as engaging and timely topics for Step 5. For the topic they choose, teachers pose questions carefully so that students problem solve about helpful (effective) and hurtful (ineffective) ways to express and regulate emotions within the selected situation.

Goals and Strategies. The questions teachers ask students to consider focus on two key components of expressing and regulating emotion: (1) the **goal** for expressing and regulating an emotion, and (2) the **strategies** to achieve that goal.

Goal. We use the acronym PRIME to represent different expression and regulation goals:

Prevent
Reduce
Initiate
Maintain
Enhance

In a given situation, a character or person will want to prevent or reduce an unwanted emotion (often feelings like anger, frustration, or guilt), or initiate, maintain, or enhance a desired emotion (often feelings like joy, contentment, and excitement). Table 2.5 shows an example situation for each PRIME goal.

Table 2.5. Example of PRIME goals.

Prevent an unwanted emotion	Students may perform better if they can prevent *anxiety* before a test.
Reduce an unwanted emotion	If a student is *enraged* because of a fight with another student, reducing those feelings may help her to behave appropriately in class.
Initiate a desired emotion	Sports performance may improve if team members initiate feelings of *optimism* before a sporting event.
Maintain a desired emotion	Maintaining feelings of *pride* may boost a student's self-esteem.
Enhance a desired emotion	As a vacation is approaching, students may want to enhance their feelings of *eagerness* to the level of *excitement*.

Strategies. There are many strategies people use to regulate the expression and experience of an emotion. In general, people can regulate an emotion by doing something or thinking about something. We use the term, *action strategies,* to describe the behaviors people can engage in to prevent, reduce, initiate, maintain, or enhance emotions. Table 2.6 includes some examples of action strategies.

Thought strategies describe the things people can think about to prevent, reduce, initiate, maintain, or enhance emotions. Table 2.7 includes some examples of thought strategies.

Table 2.6. Examples of action strategies for regulating emotions.

- Asking a parent for advice on how to improve work in a subject area in order to prevent feelings of hopelessness.

- Taking deep breaths in order to reduce enraged feelings after a fight with a sibling.

- Studying hard for an exam in order to prevent anxious feelings.

Table 2.7. Examples of thought strategies for regulating emotions.

- Thinking positively about the accomplishment of a difficult task to maintain feelings of pride.

- Reflecting on things done well rather than focusing on the one or two things done poorly in order to reduce feelings of disappointment after losing a game.

- Thinking about what happened from a different perspective, such as reducing feelings of resentment toward a friend who acted rudely by thinking about what might be going on for him (maybe he just wanted to be alone, maybe something happened at home).

Both thought and action strategies are necessary for regulating the expression and experience of emotion. At certain times, some behaviors may be inappropriate, therefore we need to rely on modifying how we think about a situation in order to avoid expressing an inappropriate emotion. Other times, changing the interpretation of an event is not sufficient for reducing the emotional experience; taking action may be necessary. A verbal apology is a better way to reduce the experience of guilt for offending a friend than is reframing the event as being the fault of the friend. One is more likely to preserve a relationship by apologizing than by shifting the blame.

The Lesson. Teachers present a discussion topic to the class and help students identify an appropriate goal for regulating the emotion. For example, in the given situation does the character want to (or should the character) *prevent, reduce, initiate, maintain,* or *enhance* the emotional experience or expression? Once a PRIME goal has been identified by the class, the teacher divides the class into small groups to brainstorm different thought and action strategies to regulate the emotion.

We encourage teachers to use cooperative learning groups in Step 5 to encourage greater participation among all students. A teacher may assign half of the small groups to identify *thought* strategies for regulating the expression and experience of the emotion, and the other half of the groups to identify *action* strategies. After each group creates a list of regulation strategies, the teacher helps students form new groups so that each has representatives from the previous *thought* and *action* groups. In these new groups, students share the strategies they came up with in their original groups, and discuss whether each of the strategies would work for achieving the PRIME goal, and whether or not each strategy would be helpful (effective) or hurtful (ineffective) given the circumstances in the situation.

To conclude Step 5, the teacher reconvenes the class as a whole and guides the students in a discussion about thought and action strategies for regulating the expression and experience of the target emotion. Students consider the benefits and consequences of the different strategies and identify the best strategies within each type. Then, students consider which strategies might be most effective for them to use to regulate their own feelings. Figure 2.9 features a sample of student work for a strategy-building session focused on the word, *ecstatic*.

Figure 2.9. Sample of student work from Step 5 for the word, *ecstatic*

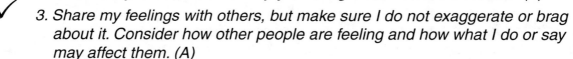

Describe topic or situation. Underline the PRIME goal.	*I'm feeling ecstatic after winning my soccer game and want to <u>maintain the feeling</u>.*

List the strategies you learned today. Put a "T" after the statement if it is a thought strategy and an "A" after the statement if it is an action strategy. Then, put a check next to the strategies that might work best for you.

     1. *Keep focused on why I was ecstatic in the first place. (T)*

     2. *Remind myself how much I enjoyed doing what made me ecstatic. (T)*

✓   3. *Share my feelings with others, but make sure I do not exaggerate or brag about it. Consider how other people are feeling and how what I do or say may affect them. (A)*

     4. *Celebrate with my friends and teammates. (A)*

     5. *When other people are ecstatic and I am not, try to be happy for them by smiling and asking them to share what happened. (A)*

✓   6. *Think positively! Don't let others' negative emotions and actions bring me down. (T)*

Explain why you checked the strategies you did:

For #3: I like sharing my enthusiasm with my friends because telling them about it makes me feel even more ecstatic—which is a great feeling!

For #6: I don't like it when my friends or family bring me down. When they do, I just ignore them and think positively.

Table 2.8 presents a summary of Step 5. Figure 2.10 provides an example of Step 5 as used in a real classroom.

Table 2.8. Summary of Step 5

1. The teacher introduces a topic to discuss for the strategy-building session.

2. The teacher leads the students in a discussion to identify the PRIME goal for expressing and regulating the emotion.

3. Students work in cooperative learning groups to brainstorm thought and action strategies for regulating the emotion.

4. The teacher reconvenes the class to discuss the proposed strategies and the extent to which each one is helpful (effective) or hurtful (ineffective) in the given situation.

5. Students reflect individually on the thought and action strategies and identify in writing the strategies that would work best for them.

Figure 2.10. Example of Step 5

In one classroom, for the word, *excluded*, students read a newspaper article about the feelings and experiences of children with physical disabilities as part of Step 2. Students wrote about the *exclusion* that children with disabilities may feel at school and in everyday life. For Step 5, the teacher asked students to imagine the following story:

> You are at a birthday party when a young girl, Jenna, suggests playing freeze tag. Everyone appears to be excited except for George who has multiple sclerosis, a disease that makes his muscles weak and his coordination so poor that he is in a wheelchair and cannot run and play certain games like the other kids. While everyone is gathering around Jenna to start the game, George lowers his head and moves his wheelchair away from the group.

The teacher asked students what the PRIME goal for George would be. After the students decided the goal should be to <u>reduce</u> George's *excluded* feelings, they split into small groups to generate specific *thought* and *action* strategies to help George feel less *excluded*.

To assist with the process, the teacher asked students to imagine that they were George. The teacher guided students through a visualization exercise to generate in them the feelings George might have had, and to think about how they would want a friend to act toward them if they were in George's situation.

During the large class discussion, the teacher asked for volunteers from each group. A student in one group said that instead of playing tag, they could choose to do something less physical like play a board game.

continued...

Another student noted that changing the activity might not necessarily make George feel less excluded because he would know that he was the reason the kids changed the activity. This student thought that changing the activity might actually make George feel more uncomfortable and isolated.

A student from a different group then suggested asking George what position he would like to play in the game or recommending different ways he could participate such as keeping score or being the referee.

Another student added that kids usually plan for who will be at a party and the types of activities to do during the party. This student suggested that maybe the kid throwing the party could talk to George beforehand and ask George what ideas he had for games that he would enjoy doing and how he would feel if someone wanted to play a game that would be challenging for him to play.

The teacher continued the problem-solving discussion until he felt that the students generated numerous strategies and identified the benefits and consequences of each. After the discussion, the teacher instructed students to identify and write about the strategies they thought would work best for them.

Pedagogical Significance of Step 5

Emotions are central to the human experience. They help us establish and maintain friendships and relationships with family members and motivate us to succeed and contribute to society. But emotions also can be disruptive.[8] Psychologists and educators agree that emotions are beneficial when the information they provide is attended to, understood, and managed effectively.[9-11]

Step 5 gives students the opportunity to use information about emotions in adaptive ways.

Students' abilities to identify emotion-related goals (the PRIME goals) and draw from a variety of strategies to regulate the expression and experience of emotions can have a significant impact on the quality and course of their lives. Knowing effective thought and action strategies to express and regulate emotions helps students to be successful academically and socially. Research supports these claims. Students who know how to express and regulate emotions tend to be psychologically healthy, socially competent, good performers in school, and better citizens.[10-12] The inability to express and regulate emotions is associated with numerous maladaptive outcomes, including anxiety, depression, aggressive behavior, fewer quality friendships, and poor academic performance.[10,12-16]

Step 5 also utilizes cooperative learning techniques. Students work in small groups to brainstorm thought and action strategies for regulating the expression and experience of emotion. A large number of studies confirm the strong, positive impact of cooperative learning on quality relationships, psychological health, and academic performance.[17,18]

Learning effective emotion regulation strategies in cooperative learning groups has added benefits. Working cooperatively in groups sustains students' curiosity and attention, and generates greater involvement in the learning process. When tasks are structured to encourage cooperation and interaction in the classroom, students greatly expand each other's knowledge base. Step 5 encourages students to discuss their own thoughts, feelings, experiences, and opinions as they use higher-order thinking skills to identify, analyze, compare, contrast, and evaluate the role and impact of emotions. By participating in small group brainstorming sessions and subsequent discussions, students improve their listening skills and are more empathic to their classmates. A sense of trust and bonding with others also develops, which helps students feel like they are part of a classroom family. When students feel connected to school, their teachers, and their classmates, they are more likely to engage actively in learning and achieve academic success.

Learning Objectives of Step 5

The goal of Step 5 is for students to develop a repertoire of regulation strategies for each feeling word and be able to apply the strategies in their daily lives, including thinking critically about academic material. Additionally, students will be better able to analyze the emotional experiences of story characters, historical figures, and people discussed in current events after regularly brainstorming strategies with their classmates. Students also practice oral communication and social skills in this Step by participating in cooperative learning groups. In this Step, students learn how to:
- **Contribute** ideas to brainstorming sessions;
- **Listen** to others' ideas in cooperative groups and large class discussions;
- **Encourage** others to come up with ideas, help others think critically about a situation, and praise the contributions of fellow team members;
- **Identify** weaknesses in strategies and attempt to generate additional ideas to fill gaps;
- **Ask** follow-up questions of other students or acknowledge their contributions in a positive way (smiles, nods, affirms experience);
- **Describe** several thought and action strategies for regulating a range of emotions; and
- **Identify** effective regulation strategies for themselves.

Summary

The Feeling Words Curriculum of *Emotional Literacy for Students* teaches students a rich vocabulary to describe their own feelings as well as the feelings of others who they encounter in literature, art, history, current events, and in their families. The curriculum, at the upper elementary level, is comprised of five Steps which work together to both strengthen knowledge of new vocabulary and develop students' RULER skills. The first four Steps provide students with a rich understanding of emotions as they connect the word to a personal experience (Step 1), write about the feelings and experiences of a real or fictitious person (Step 2), become familiar with the emotional experiences of family members (Step 3), and demonstrate the meaning of the feeling word through creative efforts (Step 4). These Steps focus primarily on teaching the first four RULER skills: recognizing, understanding, labeling, and expressing emotions. Finally, in Step 5, students develop a repertoire of skills and strategies to express or communicate emotions in socially acceptable ways and regulate or manage emotions to achieve goals.

Together, the Steps for each feeling word enhance student engagement, promote success in learning, and foster a positive and safe learning environment. Students learn to identify their own feelings and, by considering the perspectives of other adults and students, appreciate others' feelings. This helps students develop supportive relationships. With this knowledge and these skills, students can thrive in and out of school. In this way, a word is a world!

References: Chapter 2

1. Ryan, R. M., & Deci, E. L. (2000). Self-determination theory and the facilitation of intrinsic motivation, social development, and well-being. *American Psychologist, 55(1), 68-78.*

2. Caine, R., & Caine, G. (1994). *Making connections: Teaching and the human brain.* Menlo Park, CA: Addison-Wesley.

3. Sylwester, R. (1998). *Student brains, school issues: A collection of articles.* Arlington Heights, IL: SkyLight.

4. Smilansky, S. (1968). *The effects of sociodramatic play on disadvantaged preschool children.* New York: Wiley.

5. Freyberg, J. T. (1973). Increasing the imaginative play of urban disadvantaged kindergarten children through systematic training. In J. L. Singer (Ed.), *The child's world of make-believe* (pp. 129-154). New York: Academic Press.

6. Russ, S. W., Robins, A. L., & Christiano, B. A. (1999). Pretend play: Longitudinal prediction of creativity and affect in fantasy in children. *Creativity Research Journal, 12, 129-139.*

7. Zigler, E. F., & Bishop-Josef, S. J. (2006). The cognitive child vs. the whole child: Lessons from 40 years of Head Start. In D. G. Singer, R. M. Golinkoff & K. Hirsh-Pasek (Eds.), *Play = learning: How play motivates and enhances children's cognitive and social-emotional growth* (pp. 15-35). New York: Oxford University Press.

8. Frijda, N. H. (1988). The laws of emotion. *American Psychologist* 43(5), 349-358.

9. Mayer, J. D., & Salovey, P. (1997). What is emotional intelligence? In P. Salovey & D. J. Sluyter (Eds.), *Emotional development and emotional intelligence: Educational implications* (pp. 3-34). New York, NY: Basic Books, Inc.

10. Denham, S. A. (1998). *Emotional development in young children.* New York: Guilford Press.

11. Saarni, C. (1999). *The development of emotional competence.* New York: Guilford Press.

12. Fine, S. E., Izard, C. E., Mostow, A. J., Trentacosta, C. J., & Ackerman, B. P. (2003). First grade emotion knowledge as a predictor of fifth grade self-reported internalizing behaviors in children from economically disadvantaged families. *Development and Psychopathology, 15(2), 331-342.*

13. Eisenberg, N., Fabes, R. A., Guthrie, I. K., & Reiser, M. (2000). Dispositional emotionality and regulation: Their role in predicting quality of social functioning. *Journal of Personality and Social Psychology, 78, 136-157.*

14. Underwood, M. K. (2003). *Social aggression among girls.* New York: Guilford Press.

15. Halberstadt, A. G., Denham, S. A., & Dunsmore, J. C. (2001). Affective social competence. *Social Development, 10, 79-119.*

16. Kindlon, D., & Thompson, M. (2000). *Raising Cain: Protecting the emotional life of boys.* New York: Ballantine Books.

17. Johnson, D. W., & Johnson, R. T. (2004). The three Cs of promoting social and emotional learning. In J. E. Zins, R. P. Weissberg, M. C. Wang & H. J. Walberg (Eds.), *Building academic success on social and emotional learning: What does the research say?* (pp. 40-58). New York, NY: Teachers College Press.

18. Aronson, E., & Patnoe, S. (1997). *The jigsaw classroom: Building cooperation in the classroom (2nd ed.).* New York: Addison Wesley Longman.

Chapter 3
Emotionally Literate Teaching

Marc A. Brackett, Nicole A. Elbertson, Janet P. Kremenitzer, Bruce Alster, and David R. Caruso

As a teacher, I have come to the frightening conclusion that I am the decisive element in the classroom. It is my personal approach that creates the climate. It is my daily mood that makes the weather. As a teacher, I possess tremendous power to make a child's life miserable or joyous. I can be a tool of torture or an instrument of inspiration. I can humiliate or humor, hurt or heal. In all situations, it is my response that decides whether a crisis will be escalated or de-escalated, and a child humanized or dehumanized.[1]

Educators have always known that emotions play a key role in teaching and learning, yet few systematic efforts have been made to train teachers and educators on the skills associated with emotional literacy.[2, 3] Teacher preparation and professional development programs do not integrate emotions into "core" content areas of teaching academic subject matter, pedagogical theory, or classroom management.[4, 5] Indeed, the term "emotion" is mostly absent from mainstream literature advocating educational reform.[6] Emotions affect learning, mental and physical health, relationship quality, and both academic and work performance. Thus, incorporating emotional literacy into teacher training efforts can benefit all members of the learning community.

Some teachers are naturally gifted in dealing with their own emotions and those of their students; others become competent in these skills with experience. However, the knowledge and skills associated with emotional literacy (i.e., RULER: recognizing, understanding, labeling, expressing, and regulating emotion), are best accumulated in a structured and systematic way.[7-10] In our view, incorporating training on emotional literacy into teacher preparation programs and in-service workshops can optimize the learning environment for educators and students.[4, 11]

In this chapter, we introduce *Emotional Literacy for Educators.*[11] This professional development program is designed to cultivate educators' emotional literacy and increase their awareness of the importance of emotional literacy in the school environment. We first discuss the role of emotions in teaching, including how stress can hamper the learning environment. We then present a short overview of the framework underlying *Emotional Literacy for Educators,* providing several key questions to enhance the emotional literacy of educator. (A more thorough account of emotional literacy can be found in Brackett and Rivers.[12]) Next, we describe the *Blueprint*, a tool designed to help educators and students engage in effective problem solving about past, present, and future emotional experiences and challenging situations. Finally, we present some suggestions for reflective practice to increase emotional literacy and, in turn, educator effectiveness.

Emotions and Teaching

Teachers spend about 30% of their working time on class instruction, 25% on planning and grading coursework, and the remainder on meetings, classroom management, curriculum development, school-related leadership positions, social and welfare activities, and professional development.[13] In all of these activities, teachers confront a variety of pleasant and unpleasant emotions.[6, 14]

Many teachers report feeling happiness, pride, and satisfaction when students cooperate or succeed and when they receive support from parents, administrators, or fellow teachers.[15] The experience of positive emotions can enhance teacher health and well-being,[16] as well as self-efficacy.[14] Teachers' experience of positive emotions may also help young students adjust to school,[17] cultivate a stronger sense of community in the classroom, increase socially competent behavior in students, and enhance academic performance.[9, 18] Teachers also report that developing emotional bonds with students and understanding their emotions provides psychological rewards and helps set the foundation for teaching and learning.[19]

Unfortunately, teachers report experiencing unpleasant emotions more frequently than pleasant ones.[15] Feelings of anger or frustration are experienced most often when students interrupt classroom activities, violate rules, or behave aggressively;[15,20] colleagues or administrators are uncooperative;[21] and/or parents appear uncaring or irresponsible.[22] Another unpleasant emotion, guilt, arises from accountability demands, perfectionism, unclear boundaries of teaching, and failure to achieve goals associated with nurturing students.[23] Beginning teachers often encounter anxiety due to the complexities and uncertainties of learning to teach.[14] At some point in their careers, most teachers also face self-doubt and disenchantment about the teaching field.[24] These negative emotions and experiences can significantly impact the learning environment and the achievement of educational goals,[25] and may also reduce teachers' motivation[26] and confidence.[27]

Stress is the foremost emotional consequence of teaching. Various reports estimate the percentage of teachers experiencing occupational stress ranges from 30% to as high as 90%.[28] These rates are probably so high because of the interactive nature of teaching: it involves a significant potential for emotionally draining situations.[29, 30] Accordingly, more teachers experience stress and report work to be a source of stress than people working in other professions.[31] If not dealt with effectively, stress may lead to burnout, a state of emotional and physical exhaustion.[32, 33] Stress and burnout among teachers is an international phenomenon; this link has been found in Spain, France, Italy, the Netherlands, China, Australia, and many other countries.[34-39]

Occupational stress and teacher attrition are a concern for educators in the United States and abroad. Research indicates that between 40 and 50 percent of all teachers leave the profession within their first five years.[40] During the initial years of their career, teachers report a slow and steady increase in emotional exhaustion.[41] When teachers who are stressed or burnt out continue to teach, they are less effective in their classrooms.[28] Stress and burnout contribute to diminished professional commitment and lessen teacher's motivation to remain in the field. Specifically, among teachers stress and burnout result in low self-esteem, absenteeism, resignation, and early retirement. Other serious problems such as trouble with relationships outside of work and physical and mental illness also are common.[28, 42] Teachers who suffer from burnout offer students less information and praise, are less accepting of students' ideas, and interact less frequently with students.[28]

The RULER skills can help teachers understand and deal with the spectrum of emotions and stressful situations they experience in and outside of the classroom. Indeed, research shows that emotionally skilled individuals have better quality relationships and emotional health, are generally happier, and perform better at work than emotionally unskilled individuals.[43, 44] Formal emotional literacy training provides specific tools that enhance all five components of RULER and facilitate its application in the classroom and in various other contexts. Emotional literacy can help teachers experience less stress, handle challenging aspects of their jobs more easily, and establish positive and supportive relations with colleagues, administrators, and students. It prepares teachers for modeling healthy intrapersonal and interpersonal skills, which is important for motivating students to respect and care for each other and themselves. Importantly, emotional literacy enables teachers to manage their classrooms more effectively by creating a warm and supportive classroom climate. This is crucial because students' perception of care and support from teachers is associated with a number of important outcomes, including student effort, motivation, classroom engagement, and academic success,[9, 45-47] as well as classroom functioning and adherence to classroom rules and norms.[48] Students whose teachers give negative feedback and are not nurturing are more likely to perform poorly in school, both academically and socially.

Emotional Literacy for Educators

Highly qualified teachers need to know not only subject content, but also how to create a classroom community that encourages positive social interaction, active engagement in learning, and self-motivation.[49-52] *Emotional Literacy for Educators* addresses these goals.[11] This professional development training program is designed to help teachers increase their knowledge of emotions and use this knowledge to create a more stable, supportive, and productive environment for teaching and learning.

Emotional Literacy for Educators helps create an effective learning community in several ways. First, it helps educators develop emotional literacy skills, which directly impact teaching and learning. For example, teachers are encouraged to express a range of emotions in the classroom. When teachers demonstrate genuine feelings, students feel that it is safe and acceptable to experience the full range of emotions. Second, teachers learn to nurture students' self-motivation by validating students' thoughts and feelings, which triggers their passion for learning, and gets them emotionally involved in and connected to the learning process. Third, *Emotional Literacy for Educators* offers teachers guidance on how to use emotions to enhance learning of academic material. Students experience a range of emotions throughout the school day, both positive (e.g., joy due to the birth of a new sibling; pride after winning a tournament) and negative (e.g., anxiety over a fight with a friend, fear about being teased or bullied). Experiencing emotions impacts students' ability to learn and engage in classroom activities. It is difficult, if not impossible, for students to process information when they are emotionally "unready" to learn. Thus, *Emotional Literacy for Educators* provides teachers with numerous strategies for managing their students' emotional states, which optimizes attention, memory, and learning. In sum, the tools presented in the program are designed to enhance decision making, classroom management, stress management, leadership skills, interactions with students, parents, colleagues, and administrators, and general effectiveness.

In the remainder of this chapter, we present a brief sampling of the information and tools that are offered in *Emotional Literacy for Educators*, including: (1) information about emotional literacy and how its five components (RULER) are related to teaching and learning; (2) journaling questions for teachers that help them evaluate their own emotional literacy; and 3) the *Blueprint*, a tool designed to help teachers and students engage in effective problem solving about past, present, and future emotional experiences and challenging situations. In theory, the components of emotional literacy (i.e., The RULER skills) are conceptually unique. However, in practice, they overlap in their everyday applications. Thus, in this chapter, we cluster the components of RULER into three areas: recognizing and labeling emotions, which both relate to identifying emotions; understanding emotions, which refers to knowing the causes and consequences of emotions; and expressing and regulating emotion, which relate to how emotions are communicated (verbally and nonverbally) and managed. The information and tools are designed to foster skills that can be applied inside and outside of work in ways that enhance professional and personal growth.

Activities for Becoming an Emotionally Literate Teacher

In this section, we provide activities for teachers who want to become more emotionally literate. Thus, we address the reader directly using the pronoun *you*.

Recognizing and Labeling Emotion

An effective teacher is attuned to students' thoughts, feelings, and desires. Paying attention to and accurately interpreting students' gestures, demeanor, expression, and body language is essential to nurturing and teaching them.[53] Furthermore, self-awareness related to differentiating among emotions and knowledge of the words to label them are the foundations for learning other social and emotional competencies.[54] Devoting adequate time and attention to fostering such emotional awareness is critical to optimizing your success as a teacher. This is accomplished by acquiring knowledge of the different indicators of specific emotions and an extensive vocabulary of emotion words. Identifying and articulating the full range of emotions can be helpful in almost any interaction with students, parents, and administrators. And, when your interactions are more positive and productive—and less stressful—you will benefit personally as well.

One way of gathering such knowledge is to: (1) attend to your own and others' emotional experiences, and (2) build your emotional vocabulary. Teachers who recognize and label their own feelings throughout the day are more likely to express themselves well in and outside of the classroom and attend to their students' emotional needs. This optimizes the learning environment. Teachers who are familiar with identifying emotions recognize counterproductive moods and emotions in themselves and their students, which enhances their capacity to manage their classrooms.[55] For instance, a teacher who recognizes that her students are lethargic after lunch may choose to start an afternoon class with an activity that engages students both physically and mentally, such as an interactive or hands-on lesson, as opposed to a routine lecture.

In order to increase your knowledge about recognizing and labeling emotions, we have identified some key questions for you to consider. These questions are designed to enhance your emotional awareness and your ability to evaluate and describe some basic emotions, including joy, sadness, disgust, fear, anger, and surprise. We also encourage you to undertake these activities for other emotions that you and your students experience.

(1) What are the facial expressions, body language, and vocal cues that you or your students display when experiencing each of the following emotions?

Joy

Face:_____

Body:_____

Voice:_____

Sadness

Face:_____

Body:_____

Voice:_____

Disgust

Face:_____

Body:_____

Voice:_____

Fear

Face:_____

Body:_____

Voice:_____

Anger

Face:_____

Body:_____

Voice:_____

Surprise

Face:_____

Body:_____

Voice:_____

(2) Emotions vary in intensity. For instance, different intensities of *admiration* might include *like* (less intense) and *love* (more intense). For each of the following emotions, list two additional terms, representing one less intense and one more intense version of the word.

Less Intense	*Emotion*	*More Intense*
_____	*Joy*	_____
_____	*Sadness*	_____
_____	*Disgust*	_____
_____	*Fear*	_____
_____	*Anger*	_____
_____	*Surprise*	_____

The ability to recognize different intensities of emotion helps teachers intervene before their students' emotions escalate to intensities that may interfere with classroom productivity.

Understanding Emotion

To interact effectively with others, it is necessary to possess a thorough understanding of both the causes and consequences of emotions in oneself and others. Knowing the specific situations that evoke certain emotions in students can prevent misunderstandings and enhance your ability to help students learn. For example, certain emotions and mood states can improve motivation, energy, interest, and attention in both you and your students. Joy and excitement have been shown to foster creativity[56] and more ambitious goal setting.[57] Anger can synchronize the brain's activities and eliminate distractions.[58] Specifically, anger can help with classroom management when teachers display controlled anger in order to focus their own and their students' attention.[15] Negative emotional states, even less intense ones, may bias the feedback you give when grading papers—increasing the likelihood of giving lower grades—while positive emotional states may do the opposite. However, a slightly negative mood state may help students engage in focused tasks like critical and analytical thinking. Other emotions can be distracting and even destructive. For instance, anxiety can reduce memory function, which impairs the ability to perform tasks.[59, 60]

Teachers who are knowledgeable about the links between emotion and academic performance are able to evoke appropriate emotions to enhance students' learning and information processing.[61] They also know that the overall success of interactions with parents, colleagues, and school administrators is affected significantly by emotions and by each person's ability to understand the emotions and the perspectives of others. A good understanding of emotions can encourage empathy, diffuse conflict, promote healthy communication, and foster a positive learning environment.

In order to advance your understanding of emotion, we have identified some key questions for you to consider. These questions encourage you to explore in detail the contexts of your own and your students' emotional experiences in order to gain a better understanding of the causes and consequences of emotions and their progression.

(1) What are some of the situations that tend to cause YOU to experience each of the following emotions when you are teaching:

Example for *Joy*:
    I feel joyful when students demonstrate an understanding of a new concept.

Joy: _____

Sadness: _____

Disgust: _____

Fear: _____

Anger: _____

Surprise: _____

(2) What are some of the situations that tend to cause YOUR STUDENTS to experience each of the following emotions:

Example for *Joy*:
    Students feel joyful when they make a sports team or get a good grade.

Joy: _____

Sadness: _____

Disgust: _____

Fear: _____

Anger: _____

Surprise: _____

Knowledge of how you and your students react emotionally to various situations can help you create and maintain a learning environment that is most conducive to your own and your students' needs.

Expressing and Regulating Emotion

Effective expression and management of emotions helps teachers achieve educational goals and sustain well-being. Accurately expressing emotions allows individuals to communicate thoughts and feelings in the intended ways. In addition, using and modeling appropriate strategies for expressing and managing emotions in different situations can improve the quality of relationships and the classroom environment. For example, when angry or frustrated, teachers often grit their teeth (many times unknowingly), which is not an effective expression or regulation strategy (and many students do pick up on these subtle behaviors). However, stepping back, taking a breath, and being aware of the voice they are using to communicate with students are effective ways for teachers to express and manage feelings of anger and frustration.[62] This demonstrates to students that anger and frustration can be managed in constructive ways in order to focus on the task at hand.

Knowledge of how to regulate others' emotions is also critical to both developing and maintaining good relationships and to classroom management. For example, knowledge of specific strategies to calm down a rambunctious student or pep up a sad student can dramatically change the dynamics of a classroom. Moreover, each time you respond positively to your own or a student's emotions in front of your class, you are modeling healthy emotion regulation strategies.

The way teachers express and regulate their own emotions can directly impact students. Janet Patti, Professor of Administration and Supervision in the Department of Curriculum and Teaching at Hunter College, writes, "Plain and simple: people respond better to those who are optimistic, empathic, trustworthy, and inspirational. Moody, highly explosive, uncaring, or pessimistic people are often avoided or feared."[54] This is especially true in the classroom. When teachers have difficulty regulating emotions (both their own and those of their students), their students tend to experience more negative emotions in class, such as sadness, shame, and guilt.[14] In contrast, teachers who constructively regulate their own and their students' emotions while teaching create a more open and effective teaching and learning environment with fewer distractions. Similarly, teachers who control their emotional reactions and handle others' feelings successfully have an easier time resolving difficult interactions with parents and administrators.

Knowledge related to emotional expression and regulation is useful in myriad ways throughout each day. Teachers can choose among several tactics in order to quiet a boisterous post-lunch crowd, psych up a lethargic class, soothe the tears of a sad student, provide emotional support to a stressed colleague, or distract themselves from strong emotions in order to focus on classroom activities. Maintaining an arsenal of emotional expression and regulation strategies is critical to effective classroom management, stress reduction, functional professional and personal relationships, and overall quality of life.

In order to expand your knowledge in this area, we have identified key questions for you to consider. These questions are designed to prompt you to think about how you and others express and regulate emotion, evaluate the effectiveness of your current strategies, and explore the possibility of implementing other approaches.

(1) What strategies do you currently use to regulate each of the following emotions that YOU experience? What could you do differently to regulate the emotions YOU feel more effectively? (Note: Strategies to regulate emotions often vary depending on the situation. For instance, regulating joy may involve doing things to sustain the feeling when at home, but may involve distracting yourself from the feeling in order to concentrate while at school.)

Example for *Joy*:
Current: *When I'm feeling joyful at school, I am sometimes distracted, but I try to focus on containing my joy and teaching my class.*

More effective: *I could try channeling my joy into a more upbeat lesson, or if I'm very distracted, I could organize an activity where students work on their own.*

Joy

Current: _____

More effective:_____

Sadness

Current:_____

More effective:_____

Disgust

Current:_____

More effective:_____

Fear

Current:_____

More effective:_____

Anger

Current:_____

More effective:_____

Surprise

Current:_____

More effective:_____

(2) What strategies do you currently use to help YOUR STUDENTS regulate each of the following emotions? What could you do differently to help YOUR STUDENTS regulate these emotions more effectively?

Example for *Joy*:
Current: *When students seem distracted and energized because they are so happy about something, I often tell them to quiet down and to focus on the class lesson.*
More effective: *I could try having students use their joy and energy to work on a creative activity or writing assignment.*

Joy
Current: _____

More effective:_____

Sadness
Current:_____

More effective:_____

Disgust
Current:_____

More effective:_____

Fear
Current:_____

More effective:_____

Anger
Current:_____

More effective:_____

Surprise
Current:_____
More effective:_____

The ability to regulate your own and your students' negative and positive emotions can help you optimize class time by minimizing the disruptiveness of distractions and unproductive emotions.

The Blueprint

The next step is to put this accumulated knowledge about RULER into practice using the *Blueprint*. The *Blueprint* helps teachers deal effectively with challenging situations, such as a phone call from an angry parent, a class disruption from a misbehaving student, or a meeting with an unsupportive administrator. The

Blueprint guides teachers through a series of problem-solving steps. Each step of the *Blueprint* represents a different area of RULER. Table 3.1 lists the *Blueprint* questions corresponding to each element of RULER and the significance of each. Then, we provide an example that demonstrates how a teacher may use the *Blueprint* to handle a situation with a difficult parent. Later in the chapter, we provide a *Blueprint* template that you can use for your own challenging situations.

Table 3.1. The *Blueprint*[11, 63]

Describe: What is the situation or problem? Making a detailed account of the situation often clarifies the problem, organizes thoughts, and provides a framework for finding a solution.

EMOTIONAL LITERACY AREA	BLUEPRINT QUESTIONS	SIGNIFICANCE
Recognize and Label	What was I feeling? What was the other person feeling?	Identifying and communicating how you feel and how you think others might feel will break down barriers to effective interactions and problem solving.
Understand	What caused me to feel this way? What caused the other person to feel this way?	Knowledge about the underlying causes of how you and others feel can help you better understand the situation.
Express and Regulate	How did I express and regulate my feelings? How did the other person express and regulate his or her feelings?	Analyzing the specific regulation strategies you and others use is vital in evaluating and planning for difficult emotional situations.

Reflect: What could I have done differently to handle the situation more effectively? How would I have liked the situation to turn out? Is there anything I can do now? Resolving a difficult situation and strategizing about how to handle a similar situation more effectively in the future involves evaluating and reflecting upon the various ways a situation could have been handled and what can be done to improve the current situation.

Blueprint Example

Mr. Brown has a meeting scheduled with a difficult mother, Mrs. Richardson, about her son's, poor academic performance. For a few months, Mr. Brown has been pushing Mrs. Richardson to provide transportation for after-school help and tutoring for her son, Billy. However, she has refused. In a prior meeting, Mrs. Richardson repeatedly blamed Mr. Brown for her son's poor grades and stormed out after being shown a copy of Billy's low test scores. In preparation for his next meeting with Mrs. Richardson, Mr. Brown decides to use the *Blueprint* to better understand his past interactions with Mrs. Richardson in order to conduct a more productive meeting next time.

The first *Blueprint* question Mr. Brown asks himself is how he and Mrs. Richardson were feeling. To do this, he thinks back to the exchange that occurred in their last meeting. He realizes that he experienced a variety of negative emotions, mostly anger and frustration. He notices Mrs. Richardson's behavior seemed to reflect frustration, disappointment, and embarrassment.

Next, Mr. Brown asks himself what may have caused each of their feelings. Mr. Brown attributes his aggravation and frustration to Mrs. Richardson's insults, her unwillingness to meet her son's needs, and his disagreement with her perspective. Then, Mr. Brown analyzes the emotions Mrs. Richardson appeared to be experiencing. He notes that showing her Billy's test scores caused her negative emotions to escalate. Mr. Brown then speculates that Mrs. Richardson's emotions may have resulted, at least in part, from an inability to control Billy's academic problems and a belief that teachers are personally responsible for their students' performance. Mr. Brown realizes his agitated state probably set off a whole series of negative thoughts in his own mind about Mrs. Richardson, including many ungrounded assumptions about her fitness as a mother and her relationship with her son. Similarly, the heightening frustration and shame Mrs. Richardson experienced may have caused her to feel defensive in response to what she saw as an attack by Mr. Brown.

Third, Mr. Brown asks himself how he and Mrs. Richardson expressed and regulated their emotions. He remembers undertaking multiple efforts to calm himself and Mrs. Richardson simultaneously, such as trying hard not to let her know he was upset, and attempting repeatedly to explain the situation to her in a calm voice. When Mrs. Richardson interrupted Mr. Brown and raised her voice, Mr. Brown stopped talking and looked at her calmly with as straight a face as he could muster. Mrs. Richardson yelled, perhaps with the initial intention of angering Mr. Brown. Then, she left the meeting abruptly, possibly to avoid losing complete control of her emotions. Mr. Brown considers that exerting self control may have required so much effort that he was unable to really listen to Mrs. Richardson or consider her point of view. In fact, his even-tempered responses may have further infuriated Billy's mother, who perhaps was seeking to evoke some sort of reaction. Mr. Brown believes her yelling and abrupt exit were inappropriate in the situation but realizes that his reaction, although appropriate in a meeting of this sort, may have intensified her inappropriate actions.

With a better understanding of his own and Mrs. Richardson's emotions, their causes, their effects, and the strategies used to deal with them, Mr. Brown reflects upon what he could have done differently to handle this situation more effectively. In planning his upcoming meeting with Mrs. Richardson, Mr. Brown intends to listen to a few minutes of soft music before the meeting, which he knows relaxes him. Next, Mr. Brown will attempt to feel the shame, frustration, and anger that Mrs. Richardson may feel in order to gain empathy for her. He will begin the meeting by briefly explaining his feelings of genuine concern for Billy in addition to his sympathy for the student and for Mrs. Richardson having to endure this difficult situation. These expressions will be heartfelt, as Mr. Brown genuinely does feel this way. As the conversation progresses, he will be careful to avoid triggering her negative emotions. In turn, the meeting is likely to proceed more productively.

Your Blueprint

Now think of a challenging situation you recently experienced that you would like to have handled more effectively or would like to handle differently next time. Use the *Blueprint* template provided in Table 3.2 to record each step of the process. After becoming familiar with the *Blueprint*, you can use it to help you problem solve about past, present, and future difficult situations. Chapter 1 discussed how to use the Blueprint with students to help them problem solve in difficult situations (e.g., bullying, cheating, disagreements, etc.).

Table 3.2. The *Blueprint*[11]

Describe: What happened?

EMOTIONAL LITERACY AREA	ME	OTHER
Recognize and Label	What was I feeling?	What was _____ feeling?
Understand	What caused me to feel this way?	What caused _____ to feel this way?
Express and Regulate	How did I express and regulate my feelings?	How did _____ express and regulate his/her feelings?

Reflect: What could I have done differently to handle the situation better? How would I have liked the situation to turn out? Is there anything I can do now to improve the situation?

Reflective Practice

Undergraduate and graduate courses that lead toward a degree in teaching emphasize the value of reflecting upon students' level of engagement during a lesson, whether the lesson's goals have been achieved, and why students behave the way they do. However, teachers are rarely instructed to think critically about their own and their students' emotions. We suggest that you engage in reflective practice to monitor the emotional aspects of your teaching as well as your lessons and other teaching strategies. Use the *Blueprint* to guide your reflective practice. At the end of each class or school day, ask yourself the following questions:

- How did my lessons and classes go today?
- What was I feeling in class? What were my students feeling?
- What caused my students and me to feel the way we did?
- What did I do to regulate my feelings? What did I do to help regulate the feelings of my students?
- What could I have done to be more effective? What might I do next time?

Routinely asking yourself these questions will help you understand how you and your students' feelings affect each other throughout the day, and how these feelings help or hamper classroom activities. Reflection can also assist you in evaluating and adjusting your instructional and classroom management techniques to increase your students' ability to focus and learn, and improve your overall success.

Conclusion

In this chapter, we introduced *Emotional Literacy for Educators,* our professional development program, and included a brief overview of the information and tools it provides. We also discussed the prevalence and importance of emotions in teaching, presented a summary of the different components of emotional literacy (i.e., RULER), and offered a set of journaling activities to develop these areas, as well as a *Blueprint* to help teachers learn from and deal with difficult interpersonal situations more effectively. Suggestions for reflection to enhance teachers' use of emotional literacy in the classroom were also provided. Please visit www.therulerapproach.org for more information on *Emotional Literacy for Educators*.

Emotional Literacy for Educators has been implemented in schools throughout the world. Feedback from teachers who have participated in the training program has been tremendously positive. Teachers generally find the concepts and the program itself to be clear, engaging, important, and beneficial to their school. Teachers who have attended the workshops and employed the program in their schools tell us the program has changed how they teach and interact with students. For example, one teacher explained the program as, "great at helping me understand why it is so important to know how children are feeling in my class." Another teacher noted that she was "saddened, frustrated, and disappointed that more teachers do not go through this training." In general, teachers using this program report improved relationships with colleagues, principals, parents, and students. For instance, a special education teacher noted that she has benefited by gaining more emotional control and becoming more sensitive to the feelings and needs of classroom teachers. Another teacher discussed how she used the *Blueprint* to work with her colleagues on dealing with her own and other teachers' feelings of sadness and anger regarding the replacement of a retiring, highly regarded principal.

Knowledge of emotion plays an integral role in peoples' daily lives, and especially in effective teaching.[43, 44, 64] With this in mind, it is essential that programs designed to cultivate and maintain emotional literacy are incorporated into educational and professional development activities for teachers. Introducing emotional literacy concepts and tools to pre-service teachers and periodically reinforcing the concepts during in-service teacher trainings help build a teaching workforce with higher emotional literacy. Most importantly, emotionally literate students and teachers will be happier and more effective at school and at home.

References: Chapter 3

1. Ginott, H. (1971). *Teacher and child.* New York: Macmillan.

2. Kremenitzer, J.P. (2005). The emotionally intelligent early childhood educator: Self-reflective journaling. *Early Childhood Education Journal, 33,* 3-9.

3. Stemler, S.E., Elliot, J.G., Grigorenko, E.L., & Sternberg, R. (2006). There's more to teaching than instruction: Seven strategies for dealing with the practical side of teaching. *Educational Studies, 32,* 101-118.

4. Kremenitzer, J.P., & Neuhaus, K. (2003, April 8). *The emotionally intelligent teacher.* Paper presented at the National Association for the Education of Young Children, Chicago, Illinois.

5. Wilson, S.M., Floden, R.E., & Ferrini-Munday, J. (2001). T*eacher preparation research: Current knowledge, gaps, and recommendations.* Paper presented at the Center for the Study of Teaching and Policy, University of Washington, Seattle.

6. Hargreaves, A. (1998). The emotional practices of teaching. *Teaching and Teacher Education, 14,* 835-854.

7. Mills, C.J. (2003). Characteristics of effective teachers of gifted students: Teacher background and personality styles of students. *Gifted Child Quarterly, 47,* 272-281.

8. Stronge, J.H. (2002). Qualities of effective teachers. *Adolescence, 37,* 868.

9. Wentzel, K.R. (2002). Are effective teachers like good parents? Teaching styles and student adjustment in ealry adolescence. *Child Development, 73,* 287-301.

10. Brackett, M.A., & Geher, G. (2006). Measuring emotional intelligence: Paradigmatic shifts and common ground. In J. Ciarrochi, J.P. Forgas, & J.D. Mayer (Eds.), *Emotional intelligence and everyday life* (2nd ed., pp. 27-50). New York, NY: Psychology Press.

11. Brackett, M.A., & Caruso, D.R. (2007). *Emotional literacy for educators.* Cary, NC: SELmedia, Inc.

12. Brackett, M.A., & Rivers, S.E. (2011). The missing link: How emotional literacy promotes personal, academic, and social success. New York: Teachers College Press (forthcoming).

13. Campbell, R.J., & Neill, S.R. (1994). *Primary teachers at work.* London: Routledge.

14. Sutton, R.E., & Wheatley, K.F. (2003). Teachers' emotions and teaching: A review of the literature and directions for future research. *Educational Psychology Review, 15,* 327-358.

15. Emmer, E.T. (1994). Toward an understanding of the primary of classroom management and discipline. *Teaching Education, 6,* 65-69.

16. Fredrickson, B.L. (2000). Cultivating positive emotions to optimize health and well-being. *Prevention and Treatment, 3.*

17. Birch, S.H., & Ladd, G.W. (1996). Interpersonal relationships in the school environment and children's early school adjustment: The role of teachers and peers. In J. Juvenon & K. Wentzel (Eds.), *Social motivation: Understanding children's school adjustment* (pp. 199-225). New York: Cambridge University Press.

18. Schaps, E., Battistich, V., & Solomon, D. (1997). School as a caring community: A key to character education. In A. Molnar (Ed.), *Ninety-sixth yearbook of the National Society for the Study of Education* (pp. 127-139). Chicago: University of Chicago Press.

19. Woods, P., & Jeffrey, B. (1996). *Teachable moments: The art of teaching in primary schools.* Buckingham, England: Open University Press.

20. Blase, J.J. (1986). A qualitative analysis of sources of teacher stress: Consequences for performance. *American Educational Research Journal,* 23, 13-40.

21. Bullough, R.V., Knowles, J.G., & Crow, N.A. (1991). *Emerging as a teacher.* London: Routledge.

22. Lasky, S. (2000). The cultural and emotional politics of teacher-parent interactions. *Teaching and Teacher Education,* 16, 843-860.

23. Hargreaves, A., & Tucker, E. (1991). Teaching and guilt: Exploring the feelings of teaching. *Teaching and Teacher Education,* 7, 491-505.

24. Huberman, M. (1993). Steps toward a developmental model of the teaching career. In L. Kremer-Hayon, H.C. Vonk, & R. Fessler (Eds.), *Teacher professional development: A multiple perspective approach* (pp. 93-118). Amsterdam: Swets & Zeitlinger.

25. Travers, C.J. (2001). Stress in teaching: Past, present, and future. In J. Dunham (Ed.), *Stress in the workplace.* Philadelphia, PA: Whurr Publishers, Ltd.

26. Pekrun, R., Goetz, T., Titz, W., & Perry, R.P. (2002). Academic emotions in students' self-regulated learning and achievement: A program of qualitative and quantitative research. *Educational Psychologist,* 37, 91-105.

27. Kavanaugh, D.J., & Bower, G.H. (1985). Mood and self-efficacy: Impact of joy and sadness on perceived capabilities. *Cognitive Therapy Research,* 9, 507-525.

28. Travers, C.J., & Cooper, C.L. (1996). *Teachers under pressure: Stress in the teaching profession.* England: Routledge.

29. Dorman, J. (2003). Testing a model for teacher burnout. *Australian Journal of Educational and Developmental Psychology,* 3, 35-47.

30. Maslach, C., & Leiter, M.P. (1999). Teacher burnout: A research agenda. In R. Vandenberghe, A.M. Huberman, & R. Huberman (Eds.), *Understanding and preventing teacher burnout: A sourcebook of international research and practice* (pp. 295-303). Cambridge, UK: Cambridge University Press.

31. Cox, T., & Brockley, T. (1984). The experience and effects of stress in teachers. *British Educational Research Journal,* 10, 83-87.

32. Guglielmi, R., & Tatrow, K. (1998). Occupational stress, burnout, and health in teachers: A methodological and theoretical analysis. *Review of Educational Research, 68*, 61-99.

33. Vandenberghe, R., & Huberman, A.M. (1999). *Understanding and preventing teacher burnout: A sourcebook of international research and practice.* Cambridge, UK: Cambridge University Press.

34. Hart, P.M. (1994). Teacher quality of work life: Integrating work experiences, psychological distress and morale. *Journal of Occupational and Organisational Psychology, 67*, 109-132.

35. Hui, E.K.P., & Chan, D.W. (1996). Teacher stress and guidance work in Hong Kong secondary school teachers. *British Journal of Guidance and Counseling, 24*, 199-211.

36. De Heus, P., & Diekstra, R. (1999). Do teachers burn out more easily? In R. Vandenberghe, R. Huberman, & A.M. Huberman (Eds.), *Understanding and preventing teacher burnout: A sourcebook of international research and practice* (pp. 269-284). Cambridge, UK: Cambridge University Press.

37. Pisanti, R., Gagliardi, M.P., Razzino, S., & Bertini, M. (2003). Occupational stress and wellness among Italian secondary school teachers. *Psychology and Health, 18*, 523-536.

38. Pedrabissi, L., Rolland, J.P., & Santinello, M. (1993). Stress and burnout among teachers in Italy and France. *Journal of Psychology,* 529-535.

39. Duran, A., Extremera, N., & Rey, L. (2001). Burnout en profesionales de la ensenanza: Un estudio en Educacion primaria, secundaria y superior. *Revista de Psicolgia del Trabajo y de las organizaciones, 17*, 45-62.

40. Ingersoll, R.M., & Smith, T.M. (2003). The wrong solution to the teacher shortage. *Educational Leadership, 60*, 30-34.

41. Frank, A.R., & McKenzie, R. (1993). The development of burnout among special educators. *Teacher Education and Special Education, 16*, 161-170.

42. van Dick, R., & Wagner, U. (2001). Stress and strain in teaching: A structural equation approach. *British Journal of Educational, 71*, 243-259.

43. Brackett, M.A., & Salovey, P. (2004). Measuring emotional intelligence with the Mayer-Salovey-Caruso Emotional Intelligence Test (MSCEIT). In G. Geher (Ed.), *Measuring emotional intelligence: Common ground and controversy* (pp. 179-194). Happauge, NY: Nova Science Publishers, Inc.

44. Mayer, J.D., Salovey, P., & Caruso, D.R. (2004). Emotional intelligence: Theory, findings, and implications. *Psychological Inquiry, 15*, 197-215.

45. Ryan, A.M., & Patrick, H. (2001). The classroom social environment and changes in adolescents' motivation and engagement during middle school. *American Education Research Journal, 38*, 437-460.

46. Wentzel, K.R. (1994). Relations of social goal pursuit to social acceptance, classroom behavior, and perceived social support. *Journal of Educational Psychology, 86*, 173-182.

47. Wentzel, K.R. (1997). Student motivation in middle school: The role of perceived pedagogical caring. *Journal of Educational Psychology, 89*, 411-419.

48. Wentzel, K.R. (1998). Social relationships and motivation in middle school: The role of parents, teachers, and peers. *Journal of Educational Psychology, 90*, 202-209.

49. No Child Left Behind Act, PL 107-110. 2001.

50. Kohn, A. (1996). *Beyond discipline: From compliance to community.* Association for Supervision and Curriculum Development.

51. Kremenitzer, J.P., & Miller, R. (2003, June). *Special role of the early childhood practitioner: A pedagogical model for all teachers at all levels.* Paper presented at the Hawaii International Conference on Education, Honolulu, Hawaii.

52. Schmuck, R.A., & Schmuck, P. (2001). *Group processes in the classroom (8th ed.).* Boston, MA: McGraw Hill.

53. van Manen, M. (1995). On the epistemology of the reflective practice. *Teachers and Teaching: Theory and Practice, 1*.

54. Patti, J. (2006). Addressing social-emotional education in teacher education. In M.J. Elias & H. Arnold (Eds.), *The educator's guide to emotional intelligence and academic achievement* (pp. 67-75). Thousand Oaks, CA: Corwin Press.

55. Emmer, E.T., Evertson, C.M., & Anderson, L.M. (1980). Effective classroom management at the beginning of the schoolyear. *The Elementary School Journal, 80*, 219-231.

56. Fredrickson, B.L., & Branigan, C. (2005). Positive emotions broaden the scope of attention and thought-action repertoires. *Cognition and Emotion, 19*, 313-332.

57. Locke, E.A., & Lathum, G.P. (1990). Work motivation and satisfaction: Light at the end of the tunnel. *Psychological Science, 1*, 240-246.

58. LeDoux, J.E. (1996). *The emotional brain: The mysterious underpinnings of emotional life.* New York: Simon & Schuster.

59. Eysenck, M.W., & Calco, M.G. (1992). Anxiety and performance: The processing efficiency theory. *Cognition and Emotion, 6*, 409-434.

60. Ashcraft, M.H., & Kirk, E.P. (2001). The relationship among working memory, math anxiety, and performance. *Journal of Experimental Psychology, 130*, 224-237.

61. Linnenbrink, E.A., & Pintrich, P.R. (2004). Role of affect in cognitive processing in academic contexts. In D.Y. Dai & R.J. Sternberg (Eds.), *Motivation, emotion, and cognition: Integrative perspective on intellectual functioning and development* (pp. 57-87). Mahwah, NJ: Lawrence Erlbaum Associates.

62. Sutton, R.E. (2004). Teaching under high-stakes testing: Dilemmas and decisions of a teacher educator. *Journal of Teacher Education, 55*, 463-475.

63. Caruso, D.R., Mayer, J.D., & Salovey, P. (2002). Emotional intelligence and emotional leadership. In R. Riggio, S. Murphy, & F. Pirozzolo (Eds.), *Multiple intelligences and leadership* (pp. 55-74). Mahwah, NJ: Lawrence Erlbaum Associates.

64. Durlak, J.A., & Weissberg, R.P. (2005, August). *A major meta-analysis of positive youth development programs.* Paper presented at the Annual Meeting of the American Psychological Association, Washington, DC.

Chapter 4
Educating the Whole Child with Emotional Literacy: Links to Social, Emotional, and Academic Competence

Susan E. Rivers, Heather Lord, Katie A. McLaughlin, Ricardo Freyre Sandoval, Marilyn D. Carpenter, and Marc A. Brackett

"Educating the mind without educating the heart is no education at all." —Aristotle

"We cannot always build the future for our youth, but we can build our youth for the future." —Franklin D. Roosevelt

The knowledge and related skills subsumed under the RULER model of emotional literacy play a critical role in ensuring success both in and outside of the classroom. However, a sentiment still exists that social and emotional learning (SEL) programs which teach emotion knowledge and skills are tangential to core academic skills and may be difficult to integrate within our overburdened education system. Such a view is false.

The goal of this chapter is to demonstrate that SEL is foundational to students' academic performance and overall success. SEL programs can be integrated into existing school curricula without taking time or focus away from other academic areas. Beyond its proximal links with academic success, SEL facilitates the achievement of the more distal goals of education by equipping students for life, allowing them to develop to their full potential, not only as students, but also as citizens and workers in a rapidly changing society. In these ways, SEL programs that teach emotion knowledge and skills can aid schools in achieving national education goals. Scientific evidence shows that SEL is a powerful tool that helps education systems meet the challenges of national education standards and prepares students for life in a competitive society.[1]

In this chapter, we offer specific examples of how The RULER Approach to SEL contributes to local, state, and national education goals. The chapter begins with an overview of why instruction in SEL is needed in schools and why classrooms are the best place to provide it. We discuss evidence showing that emotion knowledge and its associated skills contribute to the academic achievement of elementary school students as well as their ability to develop and maintain quality social relationships, psychological and physical well-being, and later life success. Next, we describe how SEL programs can be successfully implemented in schools. We suggest four ways by which the set of programs offered within The RULER Approach—*Emotional Literacy for Students*—contributes to the aforementioned outcomes. Specifically, *Emotional Literacy for Students:* (1) creates a caring and safe learning environment for students; (2) promotes student empowerment; (3) teaches students how to adopt others' perspectives and feel empathy; and (4) cultivates critical thinking so that students are better able to analyze, synthesize, and evaluate information.

The Need for Emotional Literacy Instruction in Schools

There are many reasons emotional literacy instruction should be integrated into school curricula. In this section, we describe the three reasons we consider most compelling. First, emotional literacy may protect students from developing emotional disturbances, which are prevalent among our nation's youth. Second, emotional literacy is integral to meeting national achievement standards and to equipping students with the tools needed for short-term and long-term success. Third, emotional literacy instruction should be targeted in schools because the classroom is the ideal place to teach emotion knowledge and skills.

Prevalence of Emotional Disturbances Among Students

The incidence of emotional disturbances among our nation's youth is high. Children are using prescribed antidepressants today more than ever before.[2] Indeed, approximately one in five students experiences problems with anxiety or depression—and these rates are rising continually.[3-5] The impact of emotional disturbances spans the course of students' lives. For example, students with a history of anxiety and depression are more likely during adolescence and young adulthood to engage in risky and maladaptive behaviors, such as using illicit drugs, bullying classmates, withdrawing from friends, and disconnecting from school.[6] These behaviors are problematic both to the students themselves and to society at large, threatening the physical and psychological health of youth as well as those around them.

Emotional Literacy for Students teaches the emotion knowledge and related skills that may protect students from developing emotional disturbances, from suffering their consequences, or both. Research shows that students with greater emotional literacy tend to experience more positive emotions and have greater psychological well-being that less emotionally literate students.[7,8] Emotionally literate students, for example, are most often self-confident, self-accepting, and feel that they are in control of the environment. In contrast, students with less emotion knowledge and fewer related skills are more likely to use substances like drugs or alcohol, engage in violent behaviors, and suffer from anxiety or depression.[9-16] Emotionally literate students are aware of what causes their negative emotions and may anticipate, for example, that a classroom presentation will cause them to feel distress. Instead of being overcome by this emotion, these students identify techniques to help them regulate the distress, such as practicing the presentation in front of parents or asking a teacher for tips on how to carry out a successful presentation.

Teaching Only Math and Reading Does Not Make for an Optimal Education

The federal No Child Left Behind (NCLB) Act attempted to reform public education both by articulating clear expectations for students and teachers and by linking performance toward those expectations to incentives and consequences for states, districts, and schools.[17] Under this law, states were expected to create performance standards (e.g., basic, proficient, and advanced) as well as develop and administer corresponding tests for reading, mathematics, and science. This act stated that by the 2013-2014 school year, every student must achieve proficient or advanced levels in reading and mathematics. Every school district and each individual school also was expected to make "adequate yearly progress" (AYP) towards proficiency goals, or else be subject to "corrective action."

The intent and spirit of NCLB was to create classroom environments that were optimal for learning and teaching. In application, however, this act created an environment of high-stakes testing. Confronted by the enormous pressure to meet the standards set forth by NCLB, educators devote extraordinary amounts of time and resources to improving test scores. This environment of high-stakes testing likely damages the protective emotional connection children have to school and teachers.[18] When students do not feel connected to school, their grades slip, they become disruptive in class, and they are unlikely to aspire to higher educational goals. Struggling students are most vulnerable to the anxiety and frustrations that accompany standardized tests, and over time are likely to put forth only token effort in school.[19] In this way, the environment created by high-stakes testing may threaten crucial elements within the classroom, including the fostering of supportive relationships among students and between students and adults.[20]

The emphasis on test performance also leads to reduced instruction in other areas in which students need to thrive in order to become successful adults and good citizens. For example, a recent survey reported that approximately one-quarter of school districts reduced instructional time in science and social studies in order to devote more time to reading and math.[21] The impetus for NCLB and the preceding standards-based reform movement of the late 1980s was a growing concern over American students' ability to compete in the global economy.[22-24] However, being "proficient" in math, reading, and science only partially prepares children to participate in a competitive society. The Partnership for 21st Century Skills, a group of leading business, technology, and education organizations, notes that, "[t]here is a profound gap between the knowledge and skills most students learn in school and knowledge and skills they need in typical 21st century communities and workplaces."[25] The Collaborative for the Advancement of Social and Emotional Learning (CASEL) asserts that, in addition to reading, math and science, schools also need to teach students to be good citizens who can effectively interact with others and behave constructively.[26]

The environment of high-stakes testing undermines the education of the whole child. Classrooms that strive to meet national standards by promoting academic achievement must not neglect the emotional needs of students. Students cannot sufficiently attend to or participate in learning when they lack emotional competence and are not adjusted emotionally.[27] In a *New York Times* Op-Ed piece, Timothy Shriver and Roger Weissberg take up this very issue.[28] They write:

> "The debate over education reform has tended to divide children's learning along two axes, the emotional and the academic. We'd like to deliver some important news: The two kinds of learning are intimately connected….[P]romoting students' social and emotional skills plays a critical role in improving their academic performance."

As we explain in this chapter, emotional literacy lessons can be integrated into existing curricula in ways that enhance the learning of more traditional subject areas and achieve national achievement standards.

Classrooms are an Ideal Platform for Instruction in Emotional Literacy

Schools and classrooms provide the ideal place for emotional literacy instruction. Young people in the U.S. spend 15,000 of their most formative hours in school.[29] For many children, school provides the first opportunity for continued and stable social interactions. Thus, "teachable moments" for emotional literacy must be seized upon in schools. Moreover, it is difficult for many children to acquire emotion knowledge and develop related skills solely within the home when, more and more, both parents work outside of the home and often have multiple jobs. Research by CASEL finds that, "Schools and classrooms in which adults are nurturing, supportive, and caring furnish the best contextual opportunities for social emotional learning programs to be introduced, sustained and effectively provided."[26]

Students stand to reap significant benefits when classroom teachers integrate programs like *Emotional Literacy for Students.* A recent meta-analysis of over 200 studies reveals that the average student enrolled in an SEL program performs significantly better on achievement tests than non-participants.[1] Data from multiple studies show that children who demonstrate more emotion knowledge and skills perform better academically than children with less emotion knowledge and skills.[30-35] Why is this?

SEL programs, including *Emotional Literacy for Students,* complement existing academic curricula by teaching skills that lead to higher scholastic achievement. Emotions, particularly negative ones, such as worry, anxiety, and frustration, can interfere with learning by disrupting thinking and attention. When emotions associated with bullying, not belonging, or divorce cause students to fail, merely increasing class time, instruction, and assignments will not help. Students who feel persistent negative emotions have little mental energy left over to concentrate in and outside of class.[36] In contrast, students who effectively communicate their feelings and needs and successfully manage negative emotions are less likely to be distracted by them; they are able to conserve their mental resources for paying attention in class and focusing on assignments. SEL programs also may make students feel more engaged and connected in school.[37, 38]

Evidence shows that the knowledge and skills specified by the RULER model of emotional literacy contribute to students' social competence. Students who recognize emotions in others and understand, label, express, and effectively regulate their own emotions have good social skills, strong friendships, and are highly regarded by their peers.[39-44] Students who apply emotion knowledge behave in socially appropriate, non-aggressive ways, feel secure in their friendships, and tend to be kind and considerate of others.[45-47] In turn, these positive social outcomes enhance academic achievement. For example, compared to less emotionally literate students, emotionally literate students feel more comfortable in the school environment, receive better academic support from teachers, get more social support from peers, and develop healthier attachments to school.[48, 49]

In summary, emotional literacy is important to the development of all students, regardless of their socioeconomic status. Furthermore, the beneficiaries of formal emotional literacy instruction are many—teachers, students, classrooms, and schools. (Chapters 1 and 2 of this volume also describe the many benefits of emotional literacy instruction.) The ways in which *Emotional Literacy for Students* leads to increased school engagement and academic achievement are described later in the chapter.

Why Policy-Makers Should Take Emotional Literacy Seriously

Promoting academic, social, and personal competence and preventing risky behaviors in adolescence and early adulthood should begin early in a child's life. Thus, elementary school classrooms are the optimal place to start teaching students the skills they need to be resilient, resourceful, and confident. Emotional literacy programs also help schools meet national achievement standards. In this section, we present evidence supporting the argument that emotional literacy programs are wise short-term and long-term educational investments.

Scientific studies support the importance of emotion knowledge and skills in children's development. In our own research, we have found emotion knowledge and skills correlate with higher ratings of students' leadership skills, study skills, and their ability to adapt to changes.[50] We also found that students with greater emotion knowledge are less likely to experience problems (according to teacher evaluations) including aggression, anxiety, misconduct, hyperactivity, and learning difficulties.

Leading economists are also calling for a greater focus on non-cognitive skills. They proclaim that the greatest returns on education investments are "from nurturing children's non-cognitive skills, giving them social, emotional and behavioral benefits that lead to success later in life…"[51] James Heckman, Economics Nobel Laureate, argued that most effective interventions take place prior to elementary school, and that investing in social-emotional skills that promote motivation, perseverance and self-control is a cost-effective way to increase the quality and productivity of the workforce.[52]

For students to thrive in a competitive and rapidly changing society, it is critical for them to develop motivation, sustained attention, self-regulatory behaviors, and the social skills required for engaging in complex social interactions.[36] In fact, a national survey of employers revealed that the three capabilities most desired in entry-level workers are strong communication skills, interpersonal skills, and motivation.[53-55] This has led some experts to observe, "the preoccupation with cognition and academic 'smarts' as measured by test scores to the exclusion of social adaptability and motivation causes a serious bias in the evaluation of many human capital interventions."[52] Investments in "social skills and motivation have large payoffs in the labor market"[52] and provide the basis for building a firm foundation for future productivity.

Empirical evidence demonstrates that the academic, social, and personal correlates of emotional literacy are mutually reinforcing and lead to successful short-term and long-term outcomes.[56] Emotional literacy helps facilitate the acquisition of skills needed to meet long-term societal expectations for education, including character, responsibility, and citizenship.[57-59] In these ways, emotional literacy has the potential to foster a more productive future for citizens and society at large. Thus, programs that promote emotional literacy carry implications for enhancing both individual opportunity and national productivity.

Teaching Emotional Literacy in Your School: How and Why It Works

Incorporating emotional literacy programs into existing academic curricula can be challenging, as successful programs must incorporate several specific elements. These elements, delineated by CASEL, include linking social-emotional instruction to the standard curriculum, providing differentiated instructional procedures, building empathy, involving parents, training and supporting teachers and staff, and demonstrating quality and effectiveness through empirical evidence.[26, 60] The RULER Approach to SEL meets these standards. In particular, the classroom program, *Emotional Literacy for Students*, leverages reading, language arts, and social studies instruction to teach emotion knowledge using an innovative, multi-faceted approach. *Emotional Literacy for Students* adheres to CASEL's recommendations and complements the regular school-day curriculum. The program, which has been adopted by and tested in school districts across the United States and abroad, addresses the particular social and emotional needs of students and helps teachers create a caring and challenging classroom environment that fosters effective and enduring academic learning.[56, 60] The accompanying training program for educators, *Emotional Literacy for Educators*,[61] described in Chapter 3, provides teachers the skills and support they need to effectively implement ELS.

Emotional Literacy for Students is a language-based program that teaches emotion knowledge at an age-appropriate level. Students learn to accurately recognize, understand, and label both their own and others' emotions, appropriately express their thoughts and feelings, and effectively regulate their emotions. Next, we will describe how the program teaches emotion knowledge and skills, and the pathways by which the program leads to academic, social, and personal competence. The following section describes how *Emotional Literacy for Students* promotes these outcomes under ideal circumstances. As all educators know, a variety of factors affect the success of any learning initiative. We conclude this section by acknowledging some of the factors that may influence the effectiveness of *Emotional Literacy for Students* in promoting positive outcomes for students ("Facilitating and Impeding Factors").

How Emotional Literacy for Students Teaches Emotion Knowledge and Skills

As described in Chapters 1 and 2, one way *Emotional Literacy for Students* teaches emotion knowledge and skills is through the Feeling Words Curriculum, which, for upper elementary students, consists of five Steps: the Personal Association, the Academic and Real World Link, the School-Home Partnership, the Creative Connection, and the Strategy-Building Session. *Emotional Literacy for Students* also employs a multifaceted approach toward school-wide integration. These critical components are depicted in the left-hand side of Figure 4.1. In this section, we describe why we believe the methods used in the program are effective for teaching emotional literacy.

Figure 4.1. The Multifaceted Approach of *Emotional Literacy for Students* and the Ways it Promotes Academic and Social Success, Health, and Well-Being

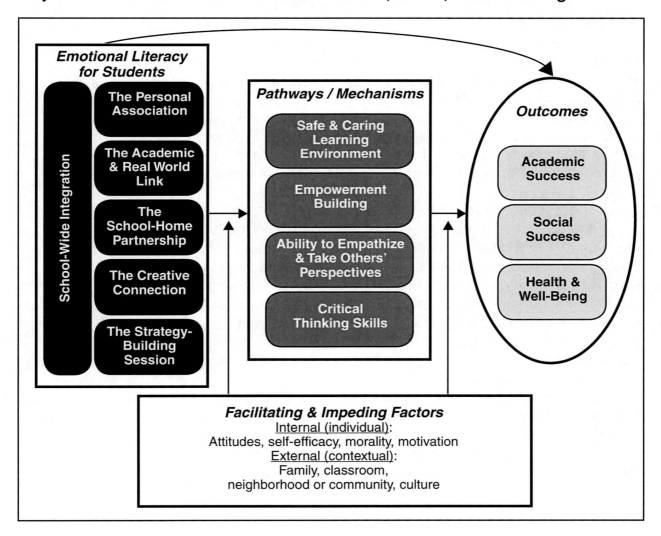

The Personal Association (Step 1)

Emotional Literacy for Students uses personalized learning to make the content of school lessons relevant to students. Each lesson begins by introducing a feeling word (i.e., *relieved, discouraged, compassion*) through personal associations. Guided by teachers, students connect each word's meaning to their own experiences. Only after students make this connection does the teacher formally introduce the word with its definition. By first identifying with the meaning of the word, students are better able to remember and integrate the word into their vocabularies.[62]

The Academic and Real World Link (Step 2)

Emotional Literacy for Students uses integrated learning to strengthen knowledge across the curriculum. In each lesson, after learning the meaning of the emotion word, students work individually and in groups, as well as with family members to apply the word to class material, real world events, and life experiences. Students link emotion concepts to multiple academic subjects (e.g., reading, social studies), domains of their lives (e.g., family, school, friendships), and the real world (e.g., current events, sports, politics). This is important because emotions link together semantically related information in the human memory.[62] By integrating lessons across the curriculum and across domains, *Emotional Literacy for Students* facilitates the development of links between ideas and subjects, which the memory would otherwise keep separate and interpret as unrelated. For example, a student who learns that a character in a novel feels oppressed and isolated may relate that lesson to material learned in a history lesson about the Jewish people and their treatment during the reign of Hitler. Using emotions to connect disparate information also allows students to transfer emotion knowledge to class material. This transformation is beneficial given that research shows people are better able to remember information that is emotional in nature.[63-65]

The School-Home Partnership (Step 3)

Parents and other caregivers play a pivotal role in the emotional development of students. Early exposure to emotional styles like warmth and compassion versus hostility impacts the emotional lives of children as well as the ways in which they regulate their own emotions.[27] The family sharing components of *Emotional Literacy for Students* encourage parents and other family members to participate in and contribute to student learning. Weekly, structured family discussions are coordinated with classroom lessons. As described elsewhere in this book, parents receive information about the benefits of emotional literacy during introductory meetings, and learn how their contributions are crucial to the success of the program. For example, lessons require students to "teach" their parents the emotion word using the same personalized learning technique used by their teacher. By "teaching" their parents, students' learning is reinforced. In talking routinely about their personal experiences related to the emotion word, students and parents interact in positive ways, learn about each other's perspectives, and connect through shared experiences.

The Creative Connection (Step 4)

Emotional Literacy for Students requires students to think about emotions in a variety of ways. In this Step, students either draw a design or create a dramatic performance using each feeling word. Students demonstrate mastery of the word by connecting verbal emotion knowledge to a creative endeavor. This strengthens understanding and fosters divergent thinking, which leads to learning that endures rather than rote memorization of vocabulary.

The Strategy-Building Session (Step 5)

Emotional Literacy for Students incorporates activities that use emotion knowledge and skills to generate strategies for regulating emotions. For each feeling word, the teacher guides students in a discussion about appropriate ways to modify their own and others' feelings. Students brainstorm about the effectiveness of specific thoughts and actions to prevent or reduce maladaptive emotions and to initiate, maintain, or enhance adaptive emotions. Discussions may focus on emotionally charged incidents that students confront frequently, including bullying, problems associated with personal responsibility (e.g., failing to complete homework), and other difficult situations. Discussing effective strategies for managing emotion as a class encourages students to take the perspectives of others into consideration when problem solving and to identify solutions that are goal oriented and prosocial.

School-Wide Integration

Emotional Literacy for Students utilizes a whole-school approach and includes tools, such as the Blueprint and the Mood Meter, which can be used by principals and teachers of all subjects. Before the program is implemented, all teachers and principals in the school attend *Emotional Literacy for Educators,* a professional development training program in which they learn about The RULER approach of emotional literacy and engage in activities to further develop their RULER skills. With this training, adults within the school are able to model emotionally literate behavior and support its development in students. In their professional development training, educators are introduced to the Mood Meter and the Blueprint, which can be used with students to discuss and overcome challenging situations or moods confronted in a class reading, a history lesson, a current event, or something that occurred among students in the classroom. By practicing this approach to problem solving across myriad domains (history, language arts, friendships, learning), students are more likely to choose behaviors that help them meet their goals, while at the same time being respectful of others.[66]

In *Emotional Literacy for Students,* students demonstrate and expand their emotion knowledge through class discussions about their personal experiences, the real world, and class material. Students engage in learning emotion-related information through writing assignments, oral presentations, art projects, music projects, and other creative tasks. Students are more likely to remember and think about class material outside of the classroom when they have the opportunity to make connections between the material, their own feelings, and their personal experiences. Evidence shows that teaching emotion knowledge in this way contributes to academic, social, and personal competence.[9] Specifically, fifth and sixth grade students whose teachers used *Emotional Literacy for Students* in the classroom for seven months had better grades in key academic areas (e.g., reading, writing, science, social studies). Teachers also rated these students as having fewer problems related to attention and learning, and as having better study skills than their peers who did not participate. Additionally, teachers rated students who had participated in the program as having better leadership and social skills, and as being less anxious, depressed, and withdrawn than non-participants.

Pathways to Student Competence

Emotional Literacy for Students helps students approach life in ways that promote learning, cultivate and maintain quality relationships, and enhance well-being, confidence and personal growth. Figure 4.1 shows that the program accomplishes these goals in at least four ways: (1) by creating a caring and safe learning environment for students; (2) by giving students a sense of empowerment; (3) by teaching students how to adopt others' perspectives and feel empathy; and (4) by cultivating critical thinking so that students can better analyze, synthesize, and evaluate information.

Creating a caring and safe learning environment. The program provides routine opportunities for teachers and parents to demonstrate that they care about students. Each lesson opens with teachers both asking students about personal experiences and sharing experiences of their own. Additionally, in each lesson, parents and family members share their experiences and learn about the student's experiences. When teachers and parents inquire about students' feelings and adopt students' perspectives, students are likely to feel important and are less likely to behave in disruptive ways in order to gain the attention of their teachers and parents.

By helping to create caring and safe learning environments, *Emotional Literacy for Students* facilitates positive emotional experiences related to classroom participation. The program also allows students to have individualized learning experiences. Positive feedback and encouragement are rewards for both engaging in the process of learning and generating creative and thoughtful responses. Unlike most academic disciplines, there are multiple correct responses to program activities. Evaluating thinking processes, instead of simply determining whether an answer is correct or incorrect, may relieve the stress and anxiety students feel over wanting to be right and to succeed. This leads to feelings of pride and excitement when students participate in class. When students are excited about participating in emotional literacy lessons, they are more likely to also participate in other subjects such as math, reading, and science.

When students connect their emotions and personal experiences to class lessons, they take pleasure in learning, even if learning is difficult. Feeling positive emotions like enjoyment, curiosity, and hope during learning is likely to increase students' motivation to exert effort in the classroom. Students who engage in effortful learning direct and focus their attention on class lessons, continue to think about the content outside of class, and process content more deeply.[67, 68] Students who are more engaged in learning are less likely to be disruptive in class, which promotes a safe and distraction-free environment for all students.

Giving students a sense of empowerment. By participating in *Emotional Literacy for Students,* students learn that emotions refer to the thoughts, feelings, and behaviors that occur in response to achievements and challenges. Importantly, they also learn to identify multiple ways of responding effectively to their emotions and to the situations that cause them. In each feeling word lesson, students work both individually and with their classmates and teachers on tasks that help them learn how to accurately recognize, understand, label, and effectively express and regulate emotions. By practicing these skills routinely through classroom discussions and other activities, students feel empowered to confront challenges independently in new situations. When students think through and respond to challenges independently—without someone else telling them how to react—they feel success and pride. These feelings are valuable because they create a sense of self-efficacy ("I can handle this") and prepare students to be self-reliant. Students who believe in themselves and their abilities are less likely to give up on difficult assignments[69, 70] and are more likely to excel academically that those that do not.[71, 72]

The RULER skills help students to cope with difficult situations. Students can generate, identify, and select effective responses when they label their emotions with accurate and specific emotion words (e.g., *joy, pride, sadness, anger, frustration*). Emotionally literate students are aware that an effective response to a situation that causes sadness is different from an effective response to a situation that causes frustration. In contrast, students who lack emotional literacy often use simple words to describe their feelings (e.g., *bad, good, okay*). These words do not allow them to direct behavior in productive ways because they are vague and general rather than specific and directed. With an expanded feelings vocabulary, students develop a repertoire of regulation strategies that they can use when they encounter new challenges.

The program also transfers the responsibility of learning onto students. Although teachers always act as hands-on guides, students readily adopt and implement the learning process delineated by the Steps. Consequently, students begin to assume responsibility for learning about emotions, which helps give them the confidence to take ownership for learning in other subjects as well.

Teaching students how to take others' perspectives and feel empathy. In classrooms that adopt *Emotional Literacy for Students,* teachers encourage students to think about topics from multiple perspectives. Classroom discussions of emotion words help students develop the ability to consider different points of view and identify alternative explanations for others' behaviors. Students learn that their own ways of thinking about and perceiving the world are sometimes similar to how their classmates think, but are also sometimes different. As a result, students are likely to be both comfortable with their own feelings and open to differences in opinion and experience. Taking others' feelings and thoughts into consideration is central to feeling empathy.

Teaching perspective-taking and empathy helps create a richer classroom environment. For example, students are able to discuss and write about characters in books and history from multiple angles, using diverse vocabulary. Discussions about an assigned book may focus on a character's feelings and the impact those feelings have on the story's plot, problems, other characters, and resolution. Students put emotion knowledge to use when they analyze the motivations of historical figures and consider how history may have been affected if that figure's feelings had been different (e.g., What if the explorer had not felt brave and courageous? What if the president did not respect leaders of other countries?). Relating to characters' feelings allows students to engage more closely with academic material.[73] Moreover, perspective-taking and empathy foster caring about classmates and teachers. When students consider how their behaviors affect others, they are less likely to behave in ways that are destructive and disruptive. Then, teachers can spend more time teaching students and less time reprimanding them.

Emotional Literacy for Students also promotes perspective-taking and empathy in social situations, which leads to social and personal competence. For example, recognizing and understanding the emotional expressions of others helps students identify opportune times to join a group, making it easier for them to enter a group and more likely that they will be accepted by the group.[44, 74] Students who do not think about how their behavior affects others are more likely to behave in antisocial ways, such as being aggressive physically (fighting), relationally (teasing, ostracizing others, revealing others' secrets, gossiping, spreading rumors), or both.[75-77] Indeed, developing and maintaining good relationships depends upon empathy. Students who are aware of their own and others' emotions feel good about helping and being nice to others. Empathetic students understand that behaving in prosocial ways makes others have positive feelings. Consequently, they are kind and considerate because they want to be, not because a teacher or parent tells them to be.[78]

Cultivating critical thinking so that students can better analyze, synthesize, and evaluate information. *Emotional Literacy for Students* cultivates critical thinking skills in multiple ways. Rather than relying on rote memorization to learn new feeling words, students integrate new terminology by connecting it to existing knowledge. Students also expand their existing knowledge base by applying what they know in new ways. For example, after connecting a feeling word to a personal experience (existing knowledge base) in Step 1, students apply that term to a real world event or a book they are reading in class (Step 2). This process promotes integrated connections between new and existing knowledge, fostering the skills necessary to analyze, synthesize, and evaluate information.

The program also encourages divergent thinking skills and creativity. For example, students utilize different modes of thinking when they develop symbolic representations of feeling words. Students also apply these new modes of thinking during strategy-building sessions in which they discover effective strategies for managing their own emotions and coping with difficult situations. For example, students may work in groups to identify ways to help a peer who feels discouraged after failing a test in an extracurricular activity (e.g., basketball, martial arts), or to identify better ways to handle conflicts between friends. Through brainstorming and evaluating multiple cognitive and behavioral strategies to manage emotional situations, students employ higher-order processes in ways that enhance critical thinking skills.

Facilitating and Impeding Factors

The model presented in Figure 4.1 acknowledges that emotional literacy may not always lead to academic and social success, and/or better health and well-being. There are many factors—both internal and external to the student—that influence whether or not students in *Emotional Literacy for Students,* or any SEL program, experience positive outcomes. We label factors that increase the likelihood that the program leads to positive outcomes "facilitating factors." One facilitating factor is self-efficacy, which refers to a student's belief in his or her ability to apply emotion knowledge. A student's self-efficacy determines whether this knowledge is applied when needed. Students who are confident in their emotion knowledge and feel capable of applying emotion skills are more likely to experience positive outcomes. Similarly, other factors related to the individual student (internal to the student) such as the student's attitude toward learning, motivation to learn, and sense of morality (i.e., his or her orientation toward doing the right thing) may facilitate (or impede) the effectiveness of the *Emotional Literacy for Students* program in promoting positive outcomes.

Among the contextual or environmental factors that may influence the likelihood of *Emotional Literacy for Students* leading to positive outcomes are a student's neighborhood, family, classroom, and culture. For example, a student who lives in a noisy neighborhood (which causes him to have disrupted sleep and impairs his ability to concentrate on learning tasks) is unlikely to reap the full benefits of the program. The student's home life is also likely to affect learning. A student who lives in a household rife with conflict or who has parents who consider school unimportant is likely to be distracted during school and may lack motivation to learn, which would impede the effectiveness of the program. In contrast, a student who lives in a supportive household and whose family values education and learning about emotion is more likely to be engaged in learning, which would facilitate the effectiveness of *Emotional Literacy for Students.* In addition, the classroom environment can enhance or limit the benefits of emotional literacy. The program will be most effective in classrooms in which teachers value the importance of learning about emotions, manage students well, and are supportive of all students. Cultural values and norms regarding emotions and learning may also act as facilitating or impeding factors (e.g., if talking about and expressing emotions are not valued, then the program's benefits will be limited).

Educating the Whole Child

At first glance the notion of incorporating SEL programs, such as *Emotional Literacy for Students,* into school districts may appear overly challenging, especially in this era of high-stakes testing. Yet, these very conditions make it more necessary than ever for administrators, teachers, policymakers, parents, and other stakeholders in the education community to take action. Integrating SEL programs into classrooms can both alleviate the stresses imposed by the high-stakes testing environment and help schools meet the intent and spirit of national achievement standards. By teaching emotion knowledge and skills, the program prepares students to be successful academically as well as to be good citizens.

In this chapter, we argued that the skills taught in *Emotional Literacy for Students* are foundational to achieving three important components of federal standards and regulations in the United States: (a) success in academics; (b) success in life, both in the short-term and in the long-term; and (c) effective teachers and classrooms. Each of these goals will help schools prepare students to successfully compete in the world's global economy.

Emotional literacy plays an integral role in daily life.[30, 58] The benefits of programs that teach emotional literacy occur both in and outside of the classroom, for both students and teachers. As discussed in this chapter, emotional literacy is an essential skill for preparing youth for life in a rapidly changing, competitive society. Schools that integrate emotional literacy programs into their classrooms report greater academic success, improved relations between teachers and students, and fewer incidences of problem behavior.[26]

While the scientific evidence supporting emotional literacy is recent and quickly accumulating, the ideas behind it reflect the wisdom of our nation's best educators. Shriver and Weissberg demonstrate this sentiment in their *New York Times* Op-Ed with the following statement:

> "What we now understand about the role of social and emotional learning in academic learning should lead us to dramatic action, but it builds on common wisdom. Good teachers know that they can't sacrifice one part of a child for another. Now they have the figures to prove it. The time has come for policy makers to help restore balance to our nation's classrooms and, in so doing, to help American children achieve their fullest potential."[28]

The accumulating scientific evidence should stir us all to action. It's time to incorporate SEL programming into our classrooms in order to more fully prepare our nation's youth for the challenging future that awaits them.

References: Chapter 4

1. Durlak, J. A., Weissberg, R. P., Dymnicki, A. B., Taylor, R. D., & Schellinger, K. B. (in press). The impact of enhancing students' social and emotional learning: A meta-analysis of school-based universal interventions. *Child Development.*

2. Delate, T., Gelenberg, A.J., Simmons, V.A., & Motheral, B.R. (2004). Trends in the use of antidepressants in a national sample of commercially insured pediatric patients, 1998-2002. *Psychiatric Services, 55,* 387-391.

3. Benjamin, R.S., Costell, E.J., & Warren, M. (1990). Anxiety disorders in a pediatric sample. *Journal of Anxiety Disorders, 4,* 293-316.

4. Kessler, R.C., & Walters, E.E. (1998). Epidemiology of DSM-III-R major depression and minor depression among adolescents and young adults in the National Comorbidity Survey. *Depression and Anxiety, 7,* 3-14.

5. Lewinsohn, P.M., Rohde, P., Seeley, J.R., & Fischer, S.A. (1993). Age-cohort changes in the occurrence of depression and other mental disorders. *Journal of Abnormal Psychology, 102,* 110-120.

6. Substance Abuse and Mental Health Services Administration (SAMHSA). (2005). *Overview of findings from the 2004 National Survey on Drug Use and Health.* Rockville, MD: Office of Applied Studies.

7. Brackett, M.A., & Mayer, J.D. (2003). Convergent, discriminant, and incremental validity of competing measures of emotional intelligence. *Personality and Social Psychology Bulletin, 29,* 1147-1158.

8. Brackett, M. A., Rivers, S. E., Reyes, M.R. & Salovey, P. (2010). Enhancing academic performance and social and emotional competence with The RULER feeling words curriculum. *Learning and Individual Differences.*

9. Turk, C.L., Heimberg, R.G., Luterek, J.A., Mennin, D.S., & Fresco, D.M. (2005). Emotion dysregulation in generalized anxiety disorder: A comparison with social anxiety disorder. *Cognitive Therapy and Research, 29,* 89-106.

10. Zeman, J.E., Shipman, K., & Suveg, C. (2002). Anger and sadness regulation: Predictions to internalizing and externalizing symptoms in children. *Journal of Clinical Child and Adolescent Psychology, 31,* 393-398.

11. Riley, H., & Schutte, N.S. (2003). Low emotional intelligence as a predictor of substance use problems. *Journal of Drug Education, 33,* 391-398.

12. Trinidad, D.R., & Johnson, C.A. (2002). The association between emotional intelligence and early adolescent tobacco and alcohol use. *Personality and Individual Differences, 32,* 95-105.

13. Trinidad, D.R., Unger, J.B., Chou, C.P., & Johnson, C.A. (2004). The protective association between emotional intelligence with psychosocial smoking risk factors for adolescents. *Personality and Individual Differences, 36,* 945-954.

14. Winters, J., Clift, R.J.W., & Dutton, D.G. (2004). An exploratory study of emotional intelligence and domestic abuse. *Journal of Family Violence, 19,* 255-267.

15. Rottenberg, J., Kasch, K.L., Gross, J.J., & Gotlib, I.H. (2002). Sadness and amusement reactivity differentially predict concurrent and prospective functioning in major depressive disorder. *Emotion, 2*, 135-146.

16. Silk, J.S., Steinberg, L., & Morris, A.S. (2003). Adolescents' emotion regulation in daily life: Links to depressive symptoms and problem behaviors. *Child Development, 74*, 1869-1880.

17. No Child Left Behind Act, PL 107-110. 2001.

18. Mulvenon, S.W., Stegman, C.E., & Ritter, G. (2005). Test anxiety: A multifaceted study of the perceptions of teachers, principals, counselors, students and parents. *International Journal of Testing, 5*, 37-61.

19. Paris, S. (1993). Four perspectives on educational assessment. *International Journal of Disability, Development and Education, 39*, 95-105.

20. Gambone, M.A., Klem, A., & Connell, J. (2002). *Finding out what matters for youth: Testing key links in a community action framework for youth development.* Philadelphia, PA: Youth Development Strategies, Inc., and Institute for Research and Reform in Education.

21. Center on Education Policy (2005) *NCLB: Narrowing the curriculum. NCLB policy brief #3.*

22. DeBray, E.H., McDermott, K.A., & Wohlstetter, P. (2005). Introduction to the special issues of federalism reconsidered: The case of No Child Left Behind Act. *Peabody Journal of Education, 80*, 1-18.

23. Jennings, J.F. (1998). Why national standards and tests? *Politics and the quest for better schools.* Thousand Oaks, CA: Sage Press.

24. National Commission on Excellence in Education. (1983). *A nation at risk: The imperative for educational reform.* Washington, D.C.: National Commission on Excellence in Education.

25. Partnership for 21st Century Skills. (2004). *A report and mile guide for 21st century skills.* Tucson, AZ: Partnership for 21st Century Skills.

26. Elias, M.J., Zins, J.E., Weissberg, R.P., Frey, K.S., Greenberg, M.T., Haynes, N.M., Kessler, R., Schwab-Stone, M.E., & Shriver, T.P. (1997). *Promoting social and emotional learning: Guidelines for educators.* Alexandria, VA: Association for Supervision and Curriculum Development.

27. Raver, C.C. (2002). Emotions matter: Making the case for the role of young children's emotional development for early school readiness. *Social Policy Report,* XVI.

28. Shriver, T.P., & Weissberg, R.P. (2005, August 16). No emotion left behind. *New York Times.*

29. Rutter, M., Maughan, B., Mortimore, P., & Outston, J. (1979). *Fifteen thousand hours: Secondary schools and their effects on children.* London: Open Books.

30. Denham, S. A. (1998). *Emotional development in young children.* New York: Guilford Press.

31. Eisenberg, N., Fabes, R.A., Guthrie, I.K., & Reiser, M. (2000). Dispositional emotionality and regulation: Their role in predicting quality of social functioning. *Journal of Personality and Social Psychology,* 78, 136-157.

32. Feldman, R.S., Philippot, P., & Custrini, R.J. (1991). Social competence and nonverbal behavior. In R.S. Feldman & B. Rime (Eds.), *Fundamentals of nonverbal behavior* (pp. 329-350). New York: Cambridge University Press.

33. Gil-Olarte Marquez, P., Palomera Martin, R., & Brackett, M.A. (2006). Relating emotional intelligence to social competence and academic achievement in high school students. *Psicothema,* 18, 118-123.

34. Halberstadt, A.G., Dunsmore, J.C., & Denham, S.A. (2001). Spinning the pinwheel, together: More thoughts on affective social competence. *Social Development,* 10, 130-136.

35. Saarni, C. (1999). *The development of emotional competence.* New York: Guilford Press.

36. Lopes, P.N., & Salovey, P. (2004). Toward a broader education: Social, emotional and practical skills. In J.E. Zins, R.P. Weissberg, M.C. Wang, & H.J. Walberg (Eds.), *Building academic success on social and emotional learning: What does the research say?* (pp. 76-93). New York, NY: Teachers College Press.

37. Christenson, S.L., & Harvey, L.H. (2004). Family-school-peer relationships: Significance for social-emotional and academic learning. In J.E. Zins, R.P. Weissberg, M.C. Wang, & H.J. Walberg (Eds.), *Building academic success on social and emotional learning: What does the research say?* (pp. 59-75). New York: Teachers College Press.

38. Stipek, D. (2005). Children as unwitting agents in their developmental pathways. In C.R. Cooper, T. Garcia Coll, T. Barko, H. Davis, & C. Chatman (Eds.), *Developmental pathways through middle childhood: Rethinking contexts and diversity as resources* (pp. 97-117). Mahwah, NJ: Lawrence Erlbaum Associates.

39. Boyatzis, C.J., & Satyaprasad, C. (1994). Children's facial and gestural decoding and encoding: Relations between skills and with popularity. *Journal of Nonverbal Behavior,* 18, 37-55.

40. Brackett, M.A., Warner, R.M., & Bosco, J.S. (2005). Emotional intelligence and relationship quality among couples. *Personal Relationships,* 12, 197-212.

41. Denham, S.A., McKinley, M., Couchoud, E.A., & Holt, R. (1990). Emotional and behavioral predictors of peer status in young preschoolers. *Child Development,* 61, 1145-1152.

42. Eisenberg, N., Fabes, R.A., Bernzweig, J., Karbon, M., Poulin, R., & Hanish, L. (1993). The relations of emotionality and regulation to preschoolers' social skills and sociometric status. *Child Development,* 64, 1418-1438.

43. Lopes, P.N., Brackett, M.A., Nezlek, J.B., Schutz, A., Sellin, I., & Salovey, P. (2004). Emotional intelligence and social interaction. *Personality and Social Psychology Bulletin,* 30, 1018-1034.

44. Nowicki, S., & Duke, M.P. (1994). Individual differences in the nonverbal communication of affect: The Diagnostic Analysis of Nonverbal Accuracy Scale. *Journal of Nonverbal Behavior,* 18, 9-35.

45. Denham, S.A., Blair, K.A., DeMulder, E., Levitas, J., Sawyer, K., Auerbach-Major, S., & Queenan, P. (2003). Preschool emotional competence: Pathway to social competence. *Child Development,* 74, 238-256.

46. Nellum-Williams, R. (1997). Educator's commentary. In P. Salovey & D.J. Sluyter (Eds.), *Emotional development and emotional intelligence* (pp. 164). New York: Basic Books.

47. Rubin, M.M. (1999). *Emotional intelligence and its role in mitigating aggression: A correlational study of the relationship between emotional intelligence and aggression in urban adolescents.* Unpublished Dissertation, Immaculata College, Immaculata, PA.

48. Agostin, R.M., & Bain, S.K. (1997). Predicting early school success with development and social skills screeners. *Psychology in the Schools,* 34, 219-228.

49. O'Neil, R., Welsh, M., Parke, R.D., Wang, S., & Strand, C. (1997). A longitudinal assessment of the academic correlates of early peer acceptance and rejection. *Journal of Clinical Child Psychology,* 26, 290-303.

50. Rivers, S.E., Brackett, M.A., Reyes, M.R., & Salovey, P. (2008, March). *Emotion skills in early adolescence: Relationships to academic and social functioning.* Paper presented at the Annual Meeting of the American Educational Research Association, New York, NY.

51. Committee for Economic Development. (2004). *A new framework for assessing the benefits of early education.* Retrieved September 18, 2006 from http://www.ced.org/publications/date.shtml

52. Heckman, J., & Masterov, D.V. (2004). *The productivity argument for investing in young children: Committee on Economic Development,* Working Paper #5.

53. Carnevale, A.P., Gainer, L.J., & Meltzer, A.S. (1988). Workplace basics: The skills employers want. *Training and Development Journal,* 42, 22-26.

54. Dowd, K., & Liedtka, J. (1994). What corporations seek in MBA hires: A survey. *The magazine of the Graduate School Admission Council,* Winter.

55. Secretary's Commission on Achieving Necessary Skills. (1991). *What work requires of schools.* Washington, DC: U.S. Department of Labor.

56. Zins, J.E., Bloodworth, M.R., Weissberg, R.P., & Walberg, H.J. (2004). The scientific base linking social and emotional learning to school success. In J.E. Zins, R.P. Weissberg, M.C. Wang, & H.J. Walberg (Eds.), *Building academic success on social and emotional learning: What does the research say?* (pp. 3-22). New York: Teachers College Press.

57. Brackett, M.A., Lopes, P.N., Ivcevic, Z., Mayer, J.D., & Salovey, P. (2004). Integrating emotion and cognition: The role of emotional intelligence. In D. Dai & R. Sternberg (Eds.), *Motivation, emotion, and cognition: Integrating perspectives on intellectual functioning* (pp. 175-194). Mahwah, NJ: Erlbaum.

58. Mayer, J.D., Salovey, P., & Caruso, D.R. (2004). Emotional intelligence: Theory, findings, and implications. *Psychological Inquiry, 15*, 197-215.

59. Sutton, R.E., & Wheatley, K.F. (2003). Teachers' emotions and teaching: A review of the literature and directions for future research. *Educational Psychology Review, 15*, 327-358.

60. Elias, M.J. (2006). The connection between academic and social emotional learning. In M.J. Elias & H. Arnold (Eds.), *The educator's guide to emotional intelligence and academic achievement.* Thousand Oaks, CA Corwin Press.

61. Brackett, M.A., & Caruso, D.R. (2007). *Emotional literacy for educators.* Cary, NC: SELmedia, Inc.

62. Bower, G.H. (1981). Mood and memory. *American Psychologist, 36*, 129-148.

63. Burke, A., Heuer, F., & Reisberg, D. (1992). Remembering emotional events. *Memory and Cognition, 20*, 277-290.

64. Cahill, L., Haier, R.J., Falon, J., Alkire, M.T., Tag, C., Keator, D., Wu, J., & McGaugh, J.L. (1996). Amygdala activity at encoding correlated with long-term, free recall of emotional information. *Proceedings of the National Academy of Sciences, 93*, 8016-8021.

65. Cahill, L., & McGaugh, J.L. (1995). A novel demonstration of enhanced memory associated with emotional arousal. *Consciousness and Cognition: An International Journal, 4*, 410-421.

66. Crick, N.R., & Dodge, K.A. (1994). A review and reformulation of social information-processing mechanisms in children's social adjustment. *Psychological Bulletin, 115*, 74-101.

67. Linnenbrink, E.A., & Pintrich, P.R. (2004). Role of affect in cognitive processing in academic contexts. In D.Y. Dai & R.J. Sternberg (Eds.), *Motivation, emotion, and cognition: Integrative perspective on intellectual functioning and development* (pp. 57-87). Mahwah, NJ: Lawrence Erlbaum Associates.

68. Pekrun, R., Goetz, T., Titz, W., & Perry, R.P. (2002). Academic emotions in students' self-regulated learning and achievement: A program of qualitative and quantitative research. *Educational Psychologist, 37*, 91-105.

69. Bandura, A. (1977). Self-efficacy: Toward a unifying theory of behavioral change. *Psychological Review 84*, 191-215.

70. Bandura, A. (1997). *Self-efficacy: The exercise of control.* New York: Freeman & Company.

71. Caprara, G.V., Barbaranelli, C., Pastorelli, C., & Cervone, D. (2004). The contribution of self-efficacy beliefs to psychosocial outcomes in adolescence: Predicting beyond global dispositional tendencies. *Personality and Individual Differences, 37*, 751-763.

72. Robbins, S.B., Lauver, K., Le, H., Davis, D., Langley, R., & Carlstrom, A. (2004). Do psychosocial and study skills factors predict college outcomes? A meta-analysis. *Psychological Bulletin 130*, 261-288.

73. Maurer, M., & Brackett, M.A. (2004). *Emotional Literacy in the Middle School: A 6-step program to promote social, emotional, & academic learning.* Port Chester, NY: National Professional Resources.

74. Denham, S.A. (1986). Social cognition, social behavior, and emotion in preschoolers: Contextual validation. *Child Development,* 57, 194-201.

75. Crick, N.R., Casas, J.F., & Mosher, M. (1997). Relational and overt aggression in preschool. *Developmental Psychology,* 33, 579-588.

76. Dodge, K.A., Price, J.M., Bachorowski, J.-A., & Newman, J.P. (1990). Hostile attributional biases in severely aggressive adolescents. *Journal of Abnormal Psychology,* 99, 385-392.

77. Simmons, R. (2002). *Odd girl out: The hidden culture of aggression in girls.* New York: Harcourt, Inc.

78. Shure, M.B. (2004). *Thinking parent, thinking child.* New York: McGraw-Hill.

Chapter 5
Integrating The RULER Approach into your School: Guidelines for Effective Implementation of the Student Programs

Nicole A. Elbertson, Susan E. Rivers, Charlene K. Voyce, and Marc A. Brackett

"The bridge between a promising idea and its impact on students is implementation."[1]

To be effective, The RULER Approach must be implemented properly. The ability of any program to achieve improvements in student behavior and performance depends on how well it is delivered.[2,3] In this chapter, we present an overview of the process schools follow to ensure the classroom program leads to the outcomes it is designed to achieve. Because this book focuses primarily on the classroom program, we will present an overview of our implementation process guidelines for *Emotional Literacy for Students* specifically. The implementation guidelines emerged from multiple sources: feedback from teachers, information from our own observations of teachers who have implemented the program, and research that documents how school-based social and emotional learning (SEL) programs can be implemented to achieve the most promising results.[4] This information has been consolidated into a process that is easy to adapt to the needs and resources of schools. Note that this chapter focuses on quality assurance strategies for the first year schools use *Emotional Literacy for Students*. However, most of these tasks can be adapted for subsequent years (e.g., communication with parents and students will be similar each year).

This chapter is directed primarily at those persons responsible for making decisions about the program—superintendents, principals, and teachers. We recommend a district- or school-wide approach to implementation, and suggest that all stakeholders be familiar with The RULER Approach and the best practices for implementing *Emotional Literacy for Students*, which are outlined this chapter.

This chapter reflects the three primary components that assure effective program implementation. The first section, *Introducing Emotional Literacy for Students,* describes ways to introduce the program to various stakeholders, including members of the board of education, teachers, parents, and students. The second section, *Preparing for Emotional Literacy for Students,* details the specific tasks that should be completed prior to implementing the program in your school or district. The final section, *Evaluating*

Implementation and Impact of Emotional Literacy for Students, suggests ways to monitor progress and assess the effects of the program in your school or district. Each section concludes with a table that briefly summarizes the information presented in that section. You can use this table as a quick reference guide and checklist as you prepare for implementing *Emotional Literacy for Students.* Throughout the chapter, we also provide various tools and other materials for program implementation.

Introducing *Emotional Literacy for Students*

Emotional Literacy for Students was designed to both enhance the social and emotional skills of students and create a more satisfying, caring, productive, and engaging learning environment. The first step toward achieving these goals is to secure district- or school-wide commitment so that various stakeholders, including the board of education, district and building-level administrators, teachers, students, and parents, are all involved.

No component of The RULER Approach can be implemented effectively without the approval, acceptance, and assistance of these key stakeholders. We suggest that members of the school community be informed of the program in a way that is customary in your district or that has been used to introduce other successful initiatives in your school. We also recommend that both administrators and teachers be trained in emotional literacy so that they have background knowledge in emotional literacy and can model the skills the students will be learning. Regardless of which group is approached first, your school will want to make sure as many stakeholders as possible are onboard.

Informing stakeholders about the benefits of *Emotional Literacy for Students* and the process for implementing a multi-year SEL curriculum will be helpful in the long term on matters such as making program-related decisions and evaluating the long-term fit of the program with your school.[5] These individuals will be more likely to support the program and help make it work when they have been part of the planning process.

Presenting to the Board of Education and District/Building-Level Administrators

In your school or district, it may be necessary to obtain approval from your board of education to adopt *The RULER Approach* and allocate funds to support its implementation. Approval from other administrators in your district, such as superintendents and principals, may also be necessary. Depending on the procedures established by your school district, there are different ways of approaching the board of education and administrators. Typically, a superintendent, assistant superintendent, principal, or curriculum coordinator makes a presentation to these stakeholders. (Oftentimes, a presentation to an individual board member precedes a presentation to the entire board.) We recommend the following steps:

1. **Request to be added to the board meeting agenda.** It is important to request this meeting as early as possible so as to ensure inclusion on the board's agenda in a timely manner. Be sure to allow yourself plenty of time to prepare the presentation.

2. **Select a presenter who can speak articulately about The RULER Approach and its fit with your school or district.** This person should be readily recognized by the board as someone who can discuss these issues authoritatively.
3. **Include the following in the presentation:**
   - A summary of The RULER Approach and the scientific evidence of its effectiveness in various areas of student behavior and performance. A sample presentation with downloadable slides can be found at *www.therulerapproach. org* under "Resources."
   - A description of the key components of the program and a brief summary of how the program is delivered.
   - The primary goals of the school district and examples of how The RULER Approach meets these goals. Identify the match between the goals of the program (enhancing social, personal, and academic ability in students) and the policies, practices, philosophies, mission statement, objectives, and concerns of your school or district.
4. **Anticipate the possible objections and concerns which board members are likely to raise and prepare responses for addressing each.** For example, to address concerns related to funding, training, and time away from academic instruction, you may discuss the availability of external funding sources and training plans, and note the instructional time that is gained when problem behaviors are reduced. It may be helpful to prepare a list of the resources your school already has access to and those you will need in order to implement The RULER Approach successfully (e.g., physical space, staff to implement the program, books for all teachers).
5. **Involve representatives from various groups in the presentation.** This shows the board that there is diverse support for the program.

Once you have identified a date for introducing the program to key decision makers, fill out Item #1 of the checklist, *Are you Ready for Emotional Literacy for Students?* (Exhibit 5.1), provided at the end of this chapter.

Communicating with Teachers

The support and success of a program depend on the ability of teaching staff to both review the program critically and participate in its implementation.[6,7] Moreover, when teachers have a firm understanding of The RULER Approach, especially *Emotional Literacy for Students* and the competencies it promotes, they generally need less follow-up instruction.[8]

In approaching teachers, it is important to point out how The RULER Approach can help them achieve their overall learning objectives, make their work with students more productive, and improve classroom management. Because each teacher will value different aspects of The RULER Approach, it is most effective to describe the full spectrum of its benefits at the outset. Information can be shared with teachers during staff meetings, grade-level or subject-area meetings, or other professional development activities.

We suggest the following strategies for informing and engaging teachers adequately before implementing the program:

1. **Provide information about the importance of SEL programs in general, and *Emotional Literacy for Students* in particular, in fostering student success.** Many students today have social and behavioral problems, difficult home situations, and daily exposure to negative influences (e.g., media reports of violence, television shows with absent or poor role models, etc.).[9] A child's school can serve as a powerful protective influence in his or her life. A summary of the scientific evidence, such as that provided in Chapter 4 of this volume, which shows how *Emotional Literacy for Students* and other SEL programs support national educational goals by teaching critical skills, can help garner support.[9,10] Even if teachers do not consider fostering social and emotional development to be part of their role in the lives of students, you can point out how meeting these needs will help students achieve academic goals.

2. **Explain that *Emotional Literacy for Students* is designed to complement and integrate easily into existing academic curricula.** As described elsewhere in this book, there are a number of ways to implement emotional literacy lessons; in general, these efforts take about one hour per week. The lessons are incorporated easily into any English language arts, health, or social studies class and serve as a vehicle for teaching traditional topics in new ways. Because the lessons are flexible, they can be rotated among different subject-specific classes so that the class time devoted to the program is divided among several subject areas.

3. **Identify ways in which *Emotional Literacy for Students* will make the lives of teachers easier.** As the biggest challenges in schools tend to be social and behavioral in nature, you may point out how *Emotional Literacy for Students* can make teaching more enjoyable and effective by preserving the time and energy necessary to address challenges as they arise throughout the school day.

4. **Involve teachers in the planning process by providing opportunities for them to make decisions related to the program.** For instance, teachers are a great resource for making decisions about which class subjects fit best with *Emotional Literacy for Students* and how best to integrate its lessons into existing curricula. Providing opportunities for teachers to participate in planning can also facilitate the selection of teachers to implement *Emotional Literacy for Students*. Those who seem most excited or knowledgeable about the program or appear highly emotionally skilled themselves are likely to be the most effective at implementation.

5. **Reassure teachers that *Emotional Literacy for Students* is an important part of the school's curriculum and that they will receive support in implementing the program.** Help teachers identify strategies for implementing the program and ways of reducing other responsibilities so that the program is not perceived as an add-on (e.g., lessons can be combined with language arts or history lessons or used as a transitional activity following lunch period).

Some school districts have designated specific staff to serve as program facilitators who support teachers in adopting *Emotional Literacy for Students* in the classroom. Program facilitators meet with teachers at regular intervals throughout the school year and coach them on ways to improve program implementation.

Once a date is set for introducing the program to teachers, fill out Item #2 of the checklist, *Are you Ready for Emotional Literacy for Students?* (Exhibit 5.1), provided at the end of this chapter.

Involving Parents

Another important group to involve as early as possible is parents. The success of *Emotional Literacy for Students* is dependent, in part, on parents being active participants and collaborators. Thus, parents must understand their role in the program and recognize how the program supports to family values.[11] Parents' concerns will need to be addressed. For example, some parents may initially be worried about their privacy. To protect privacy, communicate to parents that they should only share with their children those stories that they are comfortable being shared in the classroom during discussions.

We recommend the following strategies for informing parents and generating their interest and support:

1. **Plan a public meeting with parents several weeks before starting to use *Emotional Literacy for Students* in the classroom.** In this meeting (or at a parent/teacher conference), outline the goals and structure of *Emotional Literacy for Students*, paying special attention to the components of the program that may require parental involvement.
2. **Provide parents with a concise handout describing *Emotional Literacy for Students* so that they can refer to this information during and after the meeting.** The sample letter included at the end of this chapter provides an overview of the program's goals, structure, and parental involvement.
3. **Make sure parents know about meetings in advance and know who to contact with program-related questions and concerns.** Some parents will not feel comfortable asking questions in a group setting or may need to read the letter more carefully to understand the program better and formulate their questions; therefore, it is important for parents to have contact information on hand for when questions arise. Meeting notices should be mailed out according to the policies and procedures your school or district uses to contact parents.
4. **Address parent concerns honestly and openly.** One concern often voiced by parents (and sometimes educators) is that there is no need for SEL programming because, from their perspectives, they are already fostering their child's social and emotional development. In response to these types of concerns, it is important to review the scientific evidence/research supporting the effectiveness of *Emotional Literacy for Students* in a simple way. For

example, note that all students can benefit from an improved school climate, which arises through implementation of social development programs.[12] Also, explain that many children need systematic teaching of social and emotional competence skills, in a manner similar to the teaching of other academic topics such as math, science, and reading.[11,13]

Once you have identified a date for introducing the program to parents/families, fill out Item #3 of the checklist, *Are you Ready for Emotional Literacy for Students?* (Exhibit 5.1), provided at the end of this chapter. The RULER Approach offers a training component for adult family members, *Emotional Literacy for Families*.[14] This program series helps parents and other caregivers develop their emotional literacy skills and become informed about *Emotional Literacy for Students* so that they can support their children fully in their own development and learning.

Introducing Students to the Program

Students' understanding and opinions of *Emotional Literacy for Students* contribute significantly to the successful implementation of the program and the attainment of positive outcomes. Students may be resistant to a program that they do not understand or accept, and such resistance could hamper the success of the program. To prevent this, the program should be presented to students clearly so that they fully understand its purpose and how it fits into their school day and their lives. Once you have identified a date for introducing the program to students, fill out Item #6 of the checklist, *Are you Ready for Emotional Literacy for Students?* (Exhibit 5.1), provided at the end of this chapter.

Addressing Difficult Questions and Concerns

After receiving a general introduction, all stakeholders should be given opportunities to voice their opinions and concerns. Meetings should allow time for open dialogue. Stakeholders should be informed about whom to contact with questions. Although addressing the concerns of teachers, parents, and other key stakeholders before implementation is preferable, sometimes it is not possible. If a particular stakeholder's concern cannot adequately be addressed before starting the program, it may be appropriate to simply suggest to that person that he or she give the program a try, reminding the concerned individual that regular meetings will be scheduled to provide a forum for new or ongoing matters, and to offer social and practical support.[11] Table 5.1 outlines recommendations for introducing *Emotional Literacy for Students* to stakeholders.

Table 5.1. Introducing _Emotional Literacy for Students_ to Stakeholders

Why It Is Important
- Diverse perspectives from the school community facilitate decision making and program support.
- Open communication with stakeholders fosters their support for the program
- Stakeholder support is crucial for program success.

Presenting to the Board of Education and Other Administrators
- Request an opportunity to present the program and prepare well.
- Select a presenter.
- Include scientific research support for _Emotional Literacy for Students._
- Be prepared to address concerns raised by board members.
- Involve different stakeholder groups in the presentation.

Communicating with Teachers
- Discuss the ease with which _Emotional Literacy for Students_ can be implemented and assimilated into academic curricula.
- Describe the importance of social and emotional programs in student success.
- Identify how the program will benefit teachers.
- Give teachers opportunities to contribute to planning and decision making.
- Let them know how they will be supported.

Involving Parents
- Hold a parent meeting several weeks in advance of the start date for the program.
- Outline the goals and format of _Emotional Literacy for Students_ and provide a handout with this information.
- Provide a schedule of meetings.
- Address concerns honestly and openly.

Introducing Students to the Program
- Tell students about the program.
- Answer any questions students have.

Addressing Questions and Concerns
- Anticipate and prepare responses to address stakeholder concerns.
- Remind individuals of protocols for addressing future challenges.

Preparing for *Emotional Literacy for Students*

In addition to introducing stakeholders to *Emotional Literacy for Students* and scheduling ongoing communication, we recommend the following plan for implementing the program, which includes six primary tasks.

Task 1: Identify a Project Coordinator or a Coordinating Committee to Manage Implementation

Identify a project coordinator (or a coordinating committee of two or three individuals) to manage program-related activities, and to monitor and facilitate the program's progress and success. The project coordinator should be someone who is trusted and respected by stakeholders, and a person with whom stakeholders are comfortable interacting. Ideally, the project coordinator will be an experienced teacher who can devote time to *Emotional Literacy for Students.* (Examples of project coordinators from other schools who have implemented the program are assistant principals or directors of curriculum.) The coordinator or committee will:

1. Oversee and facilitate the development of the *Emotional Literacy for Students* implementation plan;
2. Respond to stakeholders' questions and concerns;
3. Supervise implementation on *Emotional Literacy for Students,* including observing teachers conducting lessons;
4. Monitor and record details of implementation;
5. Help teachers link *Emotional Literacy for Students* to their curriculum requirements and other school initiatives in a coordinated and complementary way. For example, many character education efforts, such as morning meetings and family involvement, go hand-in-hand with components of the program and may be adapted to be carried out in tandem with *Emotional Literacy for Students.*
6. Select a team of internal program facilitators who will work closely with teachers to help them link *Emotional Literacy for Students* to their curriculum requirements.

When possible, it is helpful for the project coordinator to consult with project coordinators from schools that have more experience implementing *Emotional Literacy for Students.* Doing so can provide valuable ideas for creating new projects, overcoming obstacles, and giving teachers feedback on using the program. See www.therulerapproach.org for more information. Once you have identified a project coordinator or committee, fill out Item #4 of the checklist, *Are you Ready for Emotional Literacy for Students?* (Exhibit 5.1), provided at the end of this chapter.

Task 2: Make a Plan for Allocating Resources to *Emotional Literacy for Students*

With the project coordinator taking the lead, a resource allocation plan should be developed, laying down how school funds, personnel, and other resources (equipment and facilities for meetings, time for training, etc.) will be used throughout the duration of the program. (If there is a question about how best to adapt a specific program component to fit a school or district's needs and available resources, the project coordinator may contact the program developers.) Once drafted, the resource allocation plan should be shared with appropriate stakeholders so that they feel comfortable that the program is sustainable and can identify opportunities to contribute.

Task 3: Delegate Responsibility for Various Program-Related Duties

In addition to a project coordinator, other individual staff members can be responsible for program-related activities such as program facilitation for teachers, communicating with various stakeholders, taking notes during meetings, and troubleshooting. In initial planning meetings, the principal, project coordinator, program facilitators, and teachers should work together to make a list of tasks, noting who will be accountable for each. These tasks may include deciding which teachers will be trained, what grade levels will receive the program, how the program facilitators will support the teachers, and who will inform parents. The project coordinator can also delegate responsibilities to staff members and follow up to ensure the tasks are accomplished. The project coordinator may use the questionnaire, *Are you Ready for Emotional Literacy for Students?* (Exhibit 5.1), provided at the end of this chapter as a guide to accomplishing and delegating program-related tasks. In addition to making the work of the project coordinator easier, delegating tasks can enhance support for *Emotional Literacy for Students* and ensure continuity when a new coordinator assumes responsibility.

Task 4: Schedule and Conduct Trainings

Successful implementation of *Emotional Literacy for Students* is dependent upon well-prepared and committed administrators and especially teachers. The training component of implementation can make or break the program's success in your school.[6] Thus, we suggest devoting significant time and energy to training.

Emotional Literacy Training. Before *Emotional Literacy for Students* is used in classrooms, we recommend that all teachers and administrators in your school or district participate in the professional development training offered within The RULER Approach. The training provides the foundational background for teaching and modeling emotional literacy to students. Most schools that implement *Emotional Literacy for Students* decide to take the district- or school-wide approach and have all teachers participate in the professional development training offered within *Emotionally Literacy for Educators,*[15] which is described in Chapter 3. This professional development series provides teachers and other educators with tools to optimize their teaching, the classroom environment, and students' academic, social, and emotional learning. *Emotional Literacy for Administrators*[16] offers leadership development for superintendents, principals, and other administrators

Emotional Literacy for Students Training. Teachers must participate in a full-day training session on *Emotional Literacy for Students,* conducted by a certified trainer. Participation in this professional development training, which provides a detailed description of the implementation process as well as the theory and goals of the program, is essential. Many schools integrate training into other professional development opportunities. For this reason, individuals responsible for scheduling professional development days should be involved in the planning process. We recommend scheduling *Emotional Literacy for Students* trainings several months in advance to ensure that sufficient time is allocated for this training within the parameters of other professional development initiatives and requirements.

Emotional Literacy for Students Manual. About one week prior to training, teachers and other staff should each receive a copy of a training manual and be encouraged to review it. A supplemental packet that corresponds to training activities is distributed during the training session. Once you have identified a date for training staff, fill out Item #5 of the checklist, *Are you Ready for Emotional Literacy for Students?* (Exhibit 5.1), provided at the end of this chapter.

Contents of Emotional Literacy for Students Training. On the day of training, teachers are introduced to the program, including its underlying theory, goals, and key components. Details of the program protocol and effective teaching strategies are covered, and teachers observe sample lessons from the trainers before working in groups to practice the lessons. Each teacher participant prepares lessons to present to the others in training. Participants and trainers observe the lessons and offer feedback and suggestions for seamless program implementation. Part of the training session is used to address teachers' questions or concerns, and to brainstorm ways to link *Emotional Literacy for Students* with their specific curricula. For example, teachers exchange ideas about which books and units fit best with each word. Before the end of the training session, teachers should receive contact information from the project coordinator(s) and a schedule of important dates related to implementation.

Options for Emotional Literacy for Students Training. There are two options for training teachers on *Emotional Literacy for Students:* (1) the program developers send a trainer or team of trainers to your school for direct staff instruction; or (2) the program developers train a small number of teachers or other key personnel from your school who, in turn, become certified to train their colleagues to implement the program. Depending on the needs of your school, either method can be appropriate and effective. Some teachers may enjoy participating in trainings with expert trainers, while others may prefer being trained by colleagues who know their school and district, and who have experience with the program.[1] Teachers who receive extensive training from program developers may serve as program facilitators and coaches for the other teachers. Having these peer coaches on site may contribute to the success of *Emotional Literacy for Students* in your school, as these individuals are likely to be sensitized to the organization and the personalities of the teachers in your school.[3]

Keep in mind that the purpose of training is for teachers to feel knowledgeable about *Emotional Literacy for Students* and confident in their ability to teach it. Therefore, trainings should clarify questions and expectations and should be as collaborative and engaging as possible, providing detailed, concrete instruction. The program developers and training staff make every effort to achieve these goals when conducting trainings, and all certified trainers are encouraged to do the same. The individual needs, interests, skill levels, and learning styles of all the teachers involved should be taken into consideration.[5] Trainers provided by the program's developers are well equipped to provide technical support and basic encouragement in order to thoroughly prepare trainers and teachers. We advise your trainers to be ready to provide the same support, while also monitoring and adjusting their behavior, presentation style, and warmth to accommodate various teachers and other individuals in your school.

Task 5: Plan for Ongoing Support and Follow-Up Meetings

Continuous contact between project coordinators, program facilitators, teachers, and the various stakeholders at your school is crucial for the success of *Emotional Literacy for Students.* Open communication and free exchange of ideas between stakeholders will help staff cope with expected and unexpected occurrences during the delivery of the program and, in turn, will increase the probability of successful implementation.[5] Meetings should have a general structure, beginning with an outline of what will be addressed in the meeting and a reminder that there will be a period for open discussion. The project coordinators or program facilitators should report on how *Emotional Literacy for Students* is being used in classrooms, including anecdotes of teacher and student experiences. They should also provide updates on any difficulties with implementation and should field questions and address concerns. Meetings between project coordinators and school administrators should allocate time to discuss any issues raised in meetings with other stakeholders that may be resolved with additional support or resources from administration, particularly when the issue affects the ability of the implementer to conduct the program well. Notes taken during meetings provide valuable documentation of the issues covered and can be helpful in future planning.

We suggest that schools create an *Emotional Literacy for Students* meeting schedule prior to implementing the program. The schedule should include monthly meetings with teachers implementing the program, regular meetings (every other month) with school administrators, and periodic meetings, as needed, with other stakeholders (i.e., parents, students). Coordinators may choose to have meetings more frequently, even weekly, during the first few months of implementation, and then less frequently as time passes and people have become more comfortable with the program. Once you have identified dates for follow-up meetings, fill out Items 7 through 9 of the checklist, *Are you Ready for Emotional Literacy for Students?* (Exhibit 5.1), provided at the end of this chapter.

Task 6: Establish a Problem-Solving Process

In addition to holding regularly scheduled meetings, the project coordinator should be accessible to staff members by email or telephone, and, if necessary, for additional in-person support meetings. Other staff members, such as program facilitators, should be available to help with concerns. It is helpful to develop a specific plan for addressing issues as they arise. The project coordinator may look to policies or procedures that are in place for other programs in order to generate ideas about what might work best for the school or district. For instance, the project coordinator may suggest that simple, non-pressing issues be brought to the table for discussion in a scheduled meeting, but that issues that require more immediate attention follow a more detailed procedure. Once you have established a plan for addressing challenges, fill out Item #10 of the checklist, *Are you Ready for Emotional Literacy for Students?* (Exhibit 5.1), provided at the end of this chapter. Table 5.2 reviews our recommendations for preparing for implementation.

Table 5.2. Preparing for *Emotional Literacy for Students* Implementation

1. Identify a project coordinator or committee to manage implementation.
   - Identify one or more teachers or administrators to act as the project coordinator.
   - The project coordinator(s) should be trusted and respected by stakeholders and have several hours per week to devote to program coordination.
   - The project coordinator(s) will be responsible for:
     —Overseeing the implementation plan;
     —Responding to questions/concerns of various stakeholders;
     —Supervising implementation and observing lessons;
     —Monitoring and recording details of implementation;
     —Helping teachers coordinate the program with academics and other programs;
     —Selecting program facilitators and coaches to work directly with teachers on implementing the program.

2. Make a plan for allocating resources to *Emotional Literacy for Students*.
   - Develop a plan for how funds, personnel, and other resources will be used.
   - Share this plan with appropriate stakeholders.

3. Delegate responsibility for program-related tasks.
   - Make a list of tasks, such as
     —Communicating with various stakeholders;
     —Taking meeting notes;
     —Troubleshooting.
   - Assign staff members to each task.

4. Schedule and conduct trainings.
   - Select dates for *Emotional Literacy for Administrators, Emotional Literacy for Educators,* and *Emotional Literacy for Students* trainings.
   - Schedule the meeting for one full day, on they day when the largest number of staff can attend.
   - Distribute program manuals to attendees at least one week in advance of the training.
   - Select the method of training (program developers versus school personnel).

5. Plan for ongoing support and follow-up meetings.
   - Begin by developing an outline of topics to be addressed.
   - Include time for open discussion.
   - Schedule monthly meetings for teachers and bimonthly meetings for administrators.
   - Plan for periodic meetings with parents and students.

6. Establish a problem-solving process.
   - Provide stakeholders with the project coordinator/committee's contact information.
   - Develop a specific plan for dealing with urgent issues.

Evaluating the Implementation and Impact of *Emotional Literacy for Students*

Monitoring the progress of *Emotional Literacy for Students* and its impact in your school is an important part of the implementation process. Feedback from staff, parents, students, and outside observers will provide ongoing information by which to assess the quality of the program and guide in-process modifications to ensure continuous improvement. Improving implementation increases the likelihood that students will derive and sustain positive outcomes. Information gained from program monitoring can also be used to determine program effectiveness and develop strategies for ensuring continued positive outcomes in upcoming years.[17] Monitoring the program's progress and impact can be done informally or formally, depending on your school's goals. It is important to keep in mind that *Emotional Literacy for Students* is designed to be a multi-year program, from kindergarten through eighth grade, and the program's effects on social and academic outcomes may be more evident over time; as students learn more, the program becomes better integrated into the school.

Informal Evaluations

In addition to serving as forums for reviewing progress and resolving concerns, meetings with stakeholders can illuminate perceptions of the program. Short surveys or questionnaires may be administered to each group of stakeholders during the regularly scheduled *Emotional Literacy for Students* meetings. These surveys may ask about stakeholder perceptions of various aspects of *Emotional Literacy for Students* and its impact, and may gauge attitudes, beliefs, and opinions about how the program is going and how others in the program seem to be responding. One-on-one interviews or small group discussions with stakeholders also provide valuable information.

Because teachers are the ones implementing *Emotional Literacy for Students,* they are particularly important sources of information. They are well acquainted with the details of the program and how it is working in their classrooms. Those developing surveys for teachers should include questions on topics such as:
- Confidence and comfort with teaching the *Emotional Literacy for Students* lessons
- General attitudes toward the program and its specific components
- The overall value of the program
- Commitment to program goals
- Belief in the efficacy of the program
- Perceptions of principal, school, parental, and community support
- Program satisfaction
- The manner in which implementation concerns are addressed

As participants in *Emotional Literacy for Students,* students are also an excellent source of information about the progress and impact of the program. Changes in students' attitudes, behaviors, and skills over the course of the program are evidence of the program's effectiveness. Those developing surveys for students should include questions such as:

- General feelings about participating in *Emotional Literacy for Students*
- Overall satisfaction with the program and its various components
- Awareness of the goals and components of the program
- Perceptions of parent and teacher enthusiasm and involvement in the program
- Would they recommend the program to other students or classes

Administrators, parents, and outside observers can also provide useful information about the progress and impact of *Emotional Literacy for Students.* Surveys for these groups may include topics similar to those listed above.

Finally, observations by a project coordinator, program facilitator, or veteran teacher with experience implementing *Emotional Literacy for Students* are particularly valuable for evaluating how the program is affecting the classroom climate. Also, completed teacher lesson sheets or student workbook pages can be made anonymous (names removed) and evaluated as an indicator of how closely teachers and students are adhering to the program. These documents, as well as meeting notes and records of all verbal and paper ratings from various stakeholders, should be collected by project coordinators, reviewed, and shared with stakeholders individually and in meetings, and kept for future reference. Having this information readily accessible is useful when discussing continuation of funds with the board of education or other administrators, and also when communicating with new teachers and parents each year about how the program works and how well it has been received by others through the years.

Formal Evaluations

Another way of monitoring *Emotional Literacy for Students* is through formal evaluation. The purpose of formal evaluation is to obtain empirical evidence that the program is working in your school and uncover the reasons why it is or is not successful. Formal evaluation provides specific feedback on how the program is delivered, how it produces change in students, and what aspects of the program are necessary to achieve such change.[17] To conduct this type of evaluation, schools need to work with a team of researchers to collect data from stakeholders. Ideally, a multi-method approach will be employed, including surveys, observer ratings, academic records, attendance records, and assessments of student and teacher skills. This type of formal evaluation can be administered through the program developers or a research institution that specializes in education-based program evaluation. Table 5.3 reviews recommendations for evaluating the implementation and impact of *Emotional Literacy for Students* in your school or district.

Table 5.3. Evaluating Program Implementation and Impact

Why It Is Important
- Information from stakeholders and observer ratings provide ongoing information on the quality of the program and its impact on students and on the school.
- Strategies can be developed for facilitating positive outcomes in upcoming years.

Informal evaluations
- Survey stakeholders in person or with anonymous surveys.
- Ask about attitudes, beliefs, and degree of satisfaction related to *Emotional Literacy for Students.*
- Review all feedback and share it with stakeholders.
- Keep all information for future reference.

Formal evaluations
- Hire researchers to collect and analyze information from stakeholders and observers to provide concrete evidence of the effectiveness of *Emotional Literacy for Students* in your school.

Summary

The three most important components of ensuring effective implementation of *Emotional Literacy for Students* are:

1. Introducing the program to all stakeholders (i.e., administrators, teachers, parents, students) and frequently informing them about the program's progress and the ways in which they can be involved.
2. Preparing for implementation by (a) identifying a project coordinator or a core committee to lead the program in your school; (b) making a plan for allocating resources to the program; (c) deciding who will be responsible for program-related tasks; (d) scheduling and conducting trainings; (e) scheduling ongoing support and follow-up meetings; (f) establishing a problem-solving process.
3. Evaluating the implementation and impact of *Emotional Literacy for Students* by informally collecting information from stakeholders or by working with the program developers or a research institution to formally assess the program.

The recommendations described in this chapter are based on our experiences with schools that have implemented *Emotional Literacy for Students* as well as scientific research on the implementation of other programs that promote SEL. Following these suggestions (and adapting them to meet the unique needs of your school or district) will facilitate the success of the program in your school. The implementation process and the support provided by stakeholders contribute to the success of *Emotional Literacy for Students* and help secure its permanent place in your school's curriculum.

Exhibit 5.1

	ARE YOU READY FOR *Emotional Literacy for Students?*
#1	An introductory meeting with key decision makers (e.g., board of education, administrators) is scheduled for: DAY/TIME: _____ PLACE:_____ NOTES:
#2	An introductory meeting with teachers is scheduled for: DAY/TIME: _____ PLACE:_____ NOTES:
#3	An introductory meeting with the parents/families of students is scheduled for: DAY/TIME: _____ PLACE:_____ NOTES:
#4	A project coordinator/committee in our school/district has been identified: NAME(S)/CONTACT INFO: _____ _____ NOTES:
#5	*Emotional Literacy for Administrators* training is scheduled for: DAY/TIME: _____ PLACE:_____ NOTES:_____ *Emotional Literacy for Educators* training is scheduled for: DAY/TIME: _____ PLACE:_____ NOTES:_____ *Emotional Literacy for Students* training is scheduled for: DAY/TIME: _____ PLACE:_____ NOTES:
#6	Students are scheduled to be introduced to *Emotional Literacy for Students* on: DAY/TIME: _____ CLASS:_____ NOTES:_____
#7	Follow-up meeting(s) with the board of education/district-level administrators is (are) scheduled for: DAY/TIME: _____ PLACE:_____ NOTES:_____ DAY/TIME: _____ PLACE:_____ NOTES:
#8	Follow-up meeting(s) with teachers/building-level administrators is (are) scheduled for: DAY/TIME: _____ PLACE:_____ NOTES:_____ DAY/TIME: _____ PLACE:_____ NOTES:
#9	Follow-up meeting(s) with parents/families is (are) scheduled for: DAY/TIME: _____ PLACE:_____ NOTES:_____ DAY/TIME: _____ PLACE:_____ NOTES:
#10	Our plan for addressing challenges is: _____ _____
NOTES:_____	
_____	

Dear teacher,

As you know, (*the name of your school or district*) is committed to helping students become healthy and productive individuals, both inside the classroom and in the community. In pursuit of this goal (*your school or district*) is adopting a program called *Emotional Literacy for Students.* This program, created specifically for elementary school students, was designed to enhance social, emotional, and academic competencies, which serve students throughout their education and their lives. *Emotional Literacy for Students* addresses each student's unique thinking and learning style. It teaches students to compare and evaluate their own and others' thoughts, feelings, and actions; understand the main idea of what they read or hear; describe events and problems; discuss ideas and experiences; and write creatively and articulately.

Emotional Literacy for Students complements academics. Hundreds of educators in the United States and abroad have conducted emotional literacy programs successfully and have responded positively, especially regarding the ease with which the program is implemented. Research conducted on students involved in these programs confirms that the program helps students develop intellectual and communication skills and positively affects academic performance. It has also been shown to decrease risk behaviors, such as smoking.

Because you will be expected to implement *Emotional Literacy for Students* in your classroom, we wanted to inform you in writing about the program in advance. Below we have summarized the program and your role.

Specifics of the program. *Emotional Literacy for Students* activities are brief, teacher-friendly, and easily incorporated into any classroom setting. They present students with learning strategies that enable them to recognize their thoughts and feelings more accurately and confidently. Emotional literacy lessons are easily incorporated into your existing language arts or social studies curriculum. The program focuses on the development of a "feelings vocabulary"—a vocabulary of "feeling words" related to emotions—as well as reading comprehension and oral and written expression. In addition to a daylong training session, you will be provided with a comprehensive teacher manual that details five "how to" steps for easy implementation. Each step can be completed in less than 15 minutes or, if you prefer, can be extended. In addition to the weekly five steps, the program features activities that allow students to work more intensely on developing their emotional literacy.

Your training. You will receive training with the creators of *Emotional Literacy for Students* (or certified trainers) on (*dates*). In your training, you will receive materials to assist you in integrating the program into your classroom. These materials include the teacher manual with illustrative lesson plans and assessment tools. There will be plenty of time during training to discuss the program and ways to incorporate *Emotional Literacy for Students* into your class.

We greatly appreciate your cooperation. Your opinions are valuable in helping us evaluate and improve the effectiveness of school curricula. An informational/training meeting for the program is scheduled for (*date of meeting*). Please bring your questions and concerns to this meeting. If you have any questions before then, please do not hesitate to contact (*name and contact information of program coordinator*).

Sincerely,
(*name of school administrator*)

References: Chapter 5

1. Dusenbury, M. L., Brannigan, R., Falco, M., & Hansen, W. B. (2003). A review of research on fidelity of implementation: Implications for drug abuse prevention in school settings. *Health Education Research,* 18, 237-256.

2. Chen, H. (1998). Theory-driven evaluations. *Advances in Educational Productivity,* 7, 15-34.

3. Graczyk, P. A., Weissberg, R. P., Payton, J. W., Elias, M. J., Greenberg, M. T., & Zins, J. E. (2000). Criteria for evaluating the quality of school-based social and emotional learning programs. In R. Bar-On & J. D. Parke (Eds.), *The handbook of emotional intelligence: Theory, development, assessment, and application at home, school and in the workplace.* San Francisco, CA: Jossey-Bass.

4. Dane, A. V., & Schneider, B. H. (1998). Program integrity in primary and early secondary prevention: Are implementation effects out of control? *Clinical Psychology Review,* 18, 23-45.

5. Greenberg, M. T., Domitrovich, C. E., Graczyk, P. A., & Zins, J. E. (2005). *The study of implementation in school-based preventive interventions: Theory, research, and practice (Volume 3).* Rockville, MD: Center for Mental Health Services, Substance Abuse and Mental Health Services Administration.

6. Lochman, J. E. (2001). Issues in prevention with school-aged children: Ongoing intervention refinement, developmental theory, prediction and moderation, and implementation and dissemination. *Prevention and Treatment,* 4, 1-7.

7. Kam, C., Greenberg, M. T., & Walls, C. T. (2003). Examining the role of implementation quality in school-based prevention using the PATHS curriculum. *Prevention Science,* 4, 55-63.

8. Consortium of the School-Based Promotion of Social Competence. (1992). Drug and alcohol prevention curricula. In J. D. Hawkins & R. F. Catalano Jr. (Eds.), *Communities that care: Action for drug abuse prevention.* San Francisco: Jossey-Bass.

9. Elias, M. J., Zins, J. E., Weissberg, R. P., Frey, K. S., Greenberg, M. T., Haynes, N. M., et al. (1997). *Promoting social and emotional learning: Guidelines for educators.* Alexandria, VA: Association for Supervision and Curriculum Development.

10. Cohen, J. (1998). *Educating hearts and minds: Social emotional learning and the passage into adolescence.* New York: Teachers College Press.

11. Elias, M. J., Bruene-Butler, L., Blum, L., & Schuyler, T. (2000). Voices from the field: Identifying and overcoming roadblocks to carrying out programs in social and emotional learning/emotional intelligence. *Journal of Educational and Psychological Consultation,* 11, 253-272.

12. Zins, J. E., Bloodworth, M. R., Weissberg, R. P., & Walberg, H. J. (2004). The scientific base linking social and emotional learning to school success. In J. E. Zins, R. P. Weissberg, M. C. Wang & H. J. Walberg (Eds.), *Building academic success on social and emotional learning: What does the research say?* (pp. 3-22). New York: Teachers College Press.

13. Brackett, M. A., & Rivers, S. E. (2011). *The Missing Link: How Emotional Literacy Promotes Personal, Academic, and Social Success.* New York: Teachers College Press (forthcoming).

14. Brackett, M. A., Caruso, D. R., Rivers, S. E., & Stern, R. (2009). *RULER for Families.* New Haven, CT: RULER Group.

15. Brackett, M. A., & Caruso, D. R. (2007). *Emotional literacy for educators.* New Haven, CT: RULER Group.

16. Brackett, M. A., & Caruso, D. R. (2007). *Emotional literacy for administrators.* New Haven, CT: RULER Group.

17. Domitrovich, C. E., & Greenberg, M. T. (2000). The study of implementation: Current findings from effective programs that prevent mental disorders in school-aged children. *Journal of Educational and Psychological Consultation,* 11, 193-221.

Teacher Educator's Afterword: The Four Ss of Quality Teaching

What is the heart of teaching? This is the question I raise at the beginning of each of the graduate methods and child development courses that I teach. As I demonstrate the whole class "presentation model" I use the advance organizer: teachers need to know a lot about their subject to be effective high quality teachers. I then proceed to discuss that at the elementary level teachers need to know a lot about many subjects. My students help me fill in all of the content areas that elementary school teachers need to know and be able to teach: language arts, mathematics, social studies, science, the arts, physical education, health education, technology etc. So, yes, indeed, teachers in elementary schools do need to know a lot about content area subjects. But, is that all they need to know as No Child Left Behind leads us to believe?

For the second time, I ask the question, "what is the heart of teaching?" And my students respond, "knowing a lot about your subject." Now I put before them a group of green, one-inch cubes all lined up in rows with one larger green cube at the front. We then discuss what this visual image might mean. The concept that some teachers might look at all of their students in a similar way eventually comes up. I then show my age by borrowing from Pete Seeger, and introducing the term, "ticky tacky boxes that all look the same." To counter this image I then pull out of my bag of tricks a full-sized replica of a human brain and then several multi-colored smaller brains (the ones that are stress relievers that can be found in most college bookstores). This second visual demonstration highlights the need for teachers to know a lot about their subjects (their students) by understanding child development and the individual developmental needs that lead to different learning styles.

It is at this point that I again ask the question: what is the heart of teaching? My students respond with knowing a lot about: (1) the content area subjects and (2) individual students through the subject study of child development. I then ask them if knowing these two areas is sufficient. This eventually leads to the realization that this is not enough because one also needs to know the third subject area: (3) pedagogy, the art and science of teaching. This, in effect, is the primary purpose of them taking an introductory methods course to learn particular teaching techniques that constitute the art and science of teaching. So, now, what is the heart of teaching? They again respond, "knowing a lot about your subject," or what I refer to as the three Ss: (1) subject of content (2) subject of development (3) subject of pedagogy.

Just when they thought it was safe to come out of the water, I inform them that there is yet one more S. This fourth S is based on knowing a lot about the: (4) subject of the self. What are one's own emotional intelligence skills and how do they impact children in the classroom? I believe that this fourth S requires awareness and specific training in order to appropriately teach children. It is a subject area that is not traditionally taught in pre-service teacher education or in in-service professional development. It is especially critical for a teacher to have this training before he/she embarks on integrating emotional literacy or any other SEL program into his/her classroom.

I have been involved in many training presentations, workshops, and publications for Teachers and Teacher Educators in developing that 4th S relating to their own inter-personal and intra-personal development that we consider the broad components of emotional intelligence. Most recently I have worked with Teachers at P.S. 43 a public elementary school in the Bronx, New York. This school is located in the poorest Congressional District in the United States and sadly also rates as the highest residential childhood asthmatic area in our country. When I began last September, what is to be a multi-year research project in the area of Teacher Emotional Intelligence development, the first area of focus was in identifying the universal stressors of teaching as well as the added ones of urban teaching. In Chapter 3 of this book we stated that stress is the foremost emotional consequence of teaching. Occupational stress found in an urban setting such as P.S. 43 begins in the morning in trying to find a parking spot on city streets that either have one hour metered maximums or alternate side of the street restrictions. Teachers are battling the public for very limited parking often ending up in surrendering to a $125 ticket for the lucky ones or having to deal with locating your car after it has been towed across the borough and under lock and key until the additional towing and storage fees are settled. This stressor is one that I have also endured. One especially needs to have strong emotional intelligence training and successful implementing skills even before entering the building.

As part of this research project at P.S. 43 I have had teachers maintain reflective emotional intelligence journals. The following excerpts are taken from the journals of ten teachers and reflect common themes that have emerged as a result of the on-going teacher training in emotional intelligence:

> "Working in a poor neighborhood of the South Bronx, we see many students coming to school with 'baggage'. It's not easy but its part of our reality and unless we, as teachers, can help students deal with the 'baggage', we can't really focus on the academics. It is a lot to handle and takes a lot of time and energy and training. We all want to help children but don't always know how. Emotional intelligence training gave us the tools to help children look at what's bothering them and find an outlet/a way to deal with the situations as well as tools for ourselves to deal with our own frustrations. This can be very stressful and some teachers can't handle it and leave the teaching profession."

"I started using terms like, 'Right now, I'm feeling..., It appears to me that you did not understand about..., or Can you explain to me why you are...?', or 'Please use feeling words to help me understand'...I started asking them to organize their thoughts and calm down, so that I could listen, to take a deep breath, to count to 5-10 and slow down their words, to reflect and think about what they were doing, and so forth...I also started to do more count downs and hold my hand up to motion them to slow down or stop... I even started using the phrases, 'Are you bullying me?', or 'are you being a bully to'...I had always talked about choices, so these new phrases were additions to phrases I used before. Also, another favorite of mine is, 'Let me understand you, are you trying to tell me that...' That one stops them short and makes them think of what they are trying to tell me. Though, I have to admit that there are those few students that no matter how you 'sugar coat' what you want to say, they are disrespectful and disruptive to the point that you have to raise your voice higher than what you want."

"Emotional intelligence training has encouraged me to notice more, for example: the tone of my class, my choice of words. I model a lot for my children. Many of the students are from underprivileged areas, it's a little tougher than it needs to be, but they have to survive and it's our responsibility to teach them. I remember what it felt like when I was a kid and others made fun of me or when I didn't know what to do."

"When I was asked to participate in this project I had mixed feelings. At the beginning I saw it as another thing we have to do, but once it started and I saw the impact it had on me and my students, then I saw it as a plus. I have learned to take a different approach with each student. I interact with each differently depending on their needs. I am learning to think before I act. Sometimes I react too quickly. In addition, I also need to train students better, if they keep reacting with the same behavior. I need to train students to use the RULER so that they could focus on how they were feeling and how the other person was feeling?"

"The work through EI allowed me to view my classroom in a different perspective. When I encountered a situation I would think, let's see where in the scale am I going to rate this emotion. What should my following actions be in order to decipher the situation on a positive note. I managed my emotions by breathing in first and thinking about the scale. Although, at times, I must admit I did not manage me emotions well by reacting too quickly."

"Having some kind of training in emotional intelligence in college would have been helpful. This type of pre-service training would affect your teaching in a positive way and can alleviate discipline problems. I saw a decrease in classroom management problems. There was less frustration. The students enjoyed the lessons and wanted to learn more and this made me feel better and it was more rewarding."

"This EI training helped – I talked with kids more about how they feel. I shared personal experiences with them: my father was never in my life, and I wanted to meet him, I was really angry –it's a void no one can fill. So I looked at my situation – absent father, very strict mom, and I noticed it was the same as some of the students."

"I learned what triggers student's emotions. I learned to be more understanding and calm. Arguing with a student is more of a power struggle and the student wants the power. I have learned not to give in to their attention seeking powers. I have learned to not react to the students. The students became a lot calmer when I didn't 'feed into' their emotional state and waited until they calmed down before discussing behavior, issue or feelings."

"Our EI work together helped me to better manage/regulate my own emotions by recognizing potentially difficult situations ahead of time; discussing it with my students and when nothing helped we can lighten up with a laugh or ignore situations and students realize that a strategy was being used."

"When I recognized my own frustration with student B I could take a deep breathe, step back and then be better able to connect with him in the process even though he did not produce the product during that session at least we could make some connection."

An additional thought for the future and an expansion of our work in this book, would be to encourage teachers (as I have required my pre-service teacher candidates to do) to keep their own journal both as they experience the process of becoming an emotionally intelligent teacher as well as when they begin to implement this practice in the classroom with our feeling words curriculum. A sharing of journal reflections by teachers at P.S. 43 during scheduled focus group periods was found to be a highly appreciated activity and one that helped to extend and strengthen each teacher's EI skills. Emotional Intelligence abilities, like other skills in life, benefit from practice and in our experience from shared discussions. The principal and two assistant principals also kept their own EI journals and reported not only personal insights about their own abilities but also how helpful it was in better understanding their teachers. This all has been seen as an avenue for creating a more productive school culture.

When Marc Brackett and Marvin Maurer asked me to review their *Emotional Literacy in the Middle School* book and to write an endorsement section (along with Roger Weissberg and Edward Zigler) for the back cover I was especially delighted. Here was a wonderful feeling words curriculum for the middle school. What I found missing was a way to insure that the teachers who were implementing this curriculum had themselves sufficient training/background to insure quality. All too often as I have walked the hallways of many elementary schools, I have been dismayed by the lack of teacher self-regulation skills. I have heard teachers screaming at a whole class of young first graders as well as berating and shaming individual students. I have seen a veteran teacher totally lose his composure and grab a student by the collar and drag that student all the way to the office. My insistence upon highlighting teacher training and quality control of that training has now been addressed in Chapter 3 of this book, Emotionally Literate Teaching, and hopefully as this training is increased we will see a corresponding decline in poor teacher behavior. If school-wide professional development can not occur, teachers can at least have this chapter for self-study and reference. I would also encourage my colleagues in pre-service teacher education programs to use this chapter, in particular, as part of teaching what I consider to be the X-factor in teacher dispositional assessment as it is part of the 4th S in self-discovery. Starting teachers off on the right path from the beginning of their training is hopefully one factor that will keep young idealistic teachers from quitting prematurely.

My second response after reviewing the Middle School book was that while this was a very important contribution to the field it was something that really had to begin much earlier in the elementary school. Why do we have to wait until middle school to have emotionally literate children and emotionally intelligent teachers? Marc and I set up a meeting with the Middle School book publishers, Helene and Robert Hanson of NPR, Inc. My role was to pitch to Helene and Robert that we needed to create a prequel for the Middle School book. This needed to be a strong pitch because at that time that book did not yet achieve a sizeable distribution. My point of why a prequel was needed was that in addition to starting earlier, this new book would also contain an important chapter on teacher training. Luckily they agreed and the long journey of developing and field testing an elementary level version curriculum began.

What is a value-added asset of our book is that any of the other SEL curricula can be used as a supplement, addition, or substitute for our curriculum while still being able to gain benefit from the remaining chapters particularly Chapter 3 on teaching with emotional intelligence which is a universal ingredient for all SEL programs. I have already implemented this "mix and match" concept at P.S. 43 where we have worked in collaboration with the Anne Frank Center USA, to bring a 10 week Anne Frank Emotional Intelligence and Aesthetic Education curriculum into the school during the Spring semester. A teaching artist from the Center worked with the children on creating special self-portraits and graphic narratives (comic-strip frames) depicting elements of personal emotional associations with the Anne Frank Diary. The children also kept personal diaries during this time. The teachers were amazed at how engaged their students were and the overall learning that was demonstrated and that spilled over into all other academic subjects. The multi-leveled approach had a profound affect on all of the children. Particularly satisfying was the strong impact it had on two classrooms for Special Needs, one labeled as Emotionally Disturbed and the other as Learning Disabled. This turned out to be a most pleasant surprise for everyone! Students who often refused to participate in class now were eagerly engaged and showed a level of motivation that they had never demonstrated before. Teachers reported the positive over-flow into the traditional academic content areas particularly in the language arts domain.

During this period of time the classroom teachers had developed additional activities for the children such as acrostic poems and creative writing assignments about the Diary and contemporary issues such as bullying. The students also worked on a final ceremonial assembly for parents and other invited guests where each class developed an original presentation about what they learned about emotional situations based on the Diary. The thought then occurred to me that the parents could become another audience for this book and the Principal agreed, that once published, to purchase several copies for each grade so that the parents could have the option of obtaining additional background information about Emotional Intelligence. I would encourage other schools to also purchase books for parents to strengthen the School-Home Partnership (our Step 3). As we will continue with the Anne Frank curriculum in the Spring, we will be adding the feeling words curriculum in the Fall semester along with another literature based SEL curriculum. This demonstrates how well this curriculum can be integrated into an elementary school program but as well as combined with other SEL curricula.

A concrete example of changing the school culture around the concept of Emotional Intelligence is the new banner that now graces the entrance of P.S. 43 which states: "P.S. 43 An Emotionally and Academically Smart School—Imagining Greatness Through the Art of Self Discovery." This reality strongly demonstrates how effective school-wide implementation can be when all of the stakeholders are on board. Chapter 5 provides a logical plan for effective implementation with quality control. Chapter 4 on Educating the Whole Child also provides a philosophical framework for all SEL programs and in essence demonstrates how critically important pathways to student competence must include emotional literacy as an integrated component.

As all good educators strive to become reflective practitioners so too have we in our writings, deliberations and emotional laboring resulting in the birth of this book and its value to teachers, students, administrators, and parents. I am also particularly excited about the impact our book will have on pre-service teacher education. I now see how pre-service teacher education can benefit in a new way by making emotional intelligence training a required component of the curriculum in becoming a teacher and thereby adjusting the first S of quality teaching (content knowledge) to also include the subject content area of emotional literacy within the broader study of emotional intelligence as well as it being the fourth S that it always was (knowledge about one self as subject). I believe the work that we have done in creating this book has greatly enriched and expanded the concept of the 4 Ss of quality teaching and has given the question: What is the Heart of Teaching?, a new and refreshing dimension.

Janet Pickard Kremenitzer, Ed.D
Department of Early Childhood and Childhood Education
Lehman College, The City University of New York

Resources Available from:
National Professional Resources, Inc.
1-800-453-7461 / www.NPRinc.com

<u>Laminated Reference Guides</u> (Published by Dude Publishing, Port Chester, NY):

Cohen, Jonathan & Elias, Maurice. *School Climate: Building Safe, Supportive and Engaging Classrooms & Schools.* 2011.

DeRoche, Edward. *Character Matters: In Classrooms, At School, At Home.* 2008.

Ditrano, Christine. *FBA and BIP (Functional Behavior Assessment & Behavior Intervention Plan).* 2010.

Dunkelblau, Ed. *Social, Emotional & Character Development (SECD): For Teahcers, For Students, For Parents.* 2008.

Hoerr, Thomas. *Multiple Intelligences: Pathways to Success.* 2010.

Shore, Kenneth, *Classroom Management: A Guide for Elementary Teachers.* 2009.

Shore, Kenneth. *An Educator's Guide to Bullying Prevention.* Revised, 2011.

Wolfe, Patricia. *The Brain Compatible Classroom.* 2010.

Wright, Jim. *RTI & Classroom Behaviors.* 2010.

<u>Books & DVDs:</u>

Bar-On, R. and Parker, J.D.A. (Eds.) *The Handbook of Emotional Intelligence.* San Francisco, CA: Jossey-Bass. 2000.

Bocchino, Rob. *Emotional Literacy: To be a Different Kind of Smart.* Thousand Oaks, CA: Corwin Press. 1999.

Brackett, M. A., & Rivers, S. E. (2010). *The Missing Link: How Emotional Literacy Promotes Personal, Academic, and Social Success.* New York: Teachers College Press (forthcoming).

Brackett, M. A., Caruso, D. R., Rivers, S. E., & Stern, R. (2009). *RULER for Families.* New Haven, CT: Emotionally Intelligent Schools.

Casbarro, Joseph. *Test Anxiety & What You Can Do About It.* Port Chester, NY: National Professional Resources, Inc. 2003.

Cohen, Jonathan (editor). *Educating Hearts and Minds: Social Emotional Learning and the Passage into Adolescence.* New York, NY: Teachers College Press, 1999.

Coles, Robert. *Moral Intelligence of Children.* New York, NY: Random House, Inc., 1997.

DeRoche, Edward F. & Williams, Mary M. *Educating Hearts & Minds.* Thousand Oaks, CA: Corwin Press, 1998.

Eleman, P. *Emotions Revealed.* New York, NY: Henry Holt & Co., 2003.

Elias, Maurice, et al. *Engaging the Resistant Child Through Computers: A Manual to Facilitate Social and Emotional Learning.* Port Chester, NY: National Professional Resources, Inc., 2001.

Elias, Maurice, et al. *EQ & IQ = Best Leadership Practices for Caring and Successful Schools.* Thousand Oaks, CA: Corwin Press, 2002.

Elias, Maurice, et al. *Promoting Social-Emotional Learning: Guidelines for Educators.* Alexandria, VA: ASCD, 1997.

Elias, Maurice & Arnold, H. (Eds.). *The Educator's Guide to Emotional Intelligence and Academic Achievement.* Thousand Oaks, CA Corwin Press.

Gardner, Howard. *Frames of Mind: The Theory of Multiple Intelligences (10th Anniversary Edition).* New York, NY: Basic Books, 1993.

Gardner, Howard. *How Are Kids Smart? Multiple Intelligences in the Classroom (Video).* Port Chester, NY: National Professional Resources, Inc., 1995.

Goleman, Daniel. *Emotional Intelligence: A New Vision for Educators (Video).* Port Chester, NY: National Professional Resources, Inc., 1996.

Goleman, Daniel. *Emotional Intelligence: Why it Matters More Than IQ.* New York, NY: Bantam Books, 1995.

Jensen, Eric. *Successful Applications of Brain-Based Learning (Two video set).* Port Chester, NY: National Professional Resources, Inc., 2000.

Jensen, Eric. *Tools for Engagement: Managing Emotional States for Learner Success.* San Diego, CA: The Brain Store, 2003.

Kagan, Spencer. *Building Character Through Cooperative Learning (Video).* National Professional Resources, Inc., 1999.

Levine, Mel. *A Mind at a Time.* New York, NY: Simon & Schuster, 2002.

Lickona, Thomas et al. *Character Education: Restoring Respect & Responsibility in Our Schools (Video).* National Professional Resources, Inc., 1996.

Lickona, Thomas. *Character Matters.* Carmichael, CA: Touchstone Books, 2004.

Pert, Candace. *Emotion: Gatekeeper to Performance (Video).* Port Chester, NY: National Professional Resources, Inc., 1999.

Pert, Candace. *Molecules of Emotion.* New York, NY: Scribner, 1997.

Project Zero. *Educating for Understanding at Harvard Graduate School of Education (Video series).* Port Chester, NY: National Professional Resources, Inc., 2002.

Salovey, Peter et al. *Optimizing Intelligences: Thinking, Emotion & Creativity (Video).* National Professional Resources, Inc., 1998.

Shelton, Claudia M. & Stern, Robin. *Understanding Emotions in the Classroom: Differentiating Teaching Strategies for Optimal Learning.* Port Chester, NY: National Professional Resources, Inc., 2004.

Shore, Kenneth. *ABC's of Bullying Prevention.* Port Chester, NY: National Professional Resources, Inc., Revised, 2011.

Sternberg, R.J. (Ed.), *The Handbook of Intelligence.* New York, NY: Cambridge University Press, 2000.

Stirling, Diane, Archibald, Georgia, McKay, Linda & Berg, Shelley. *Character Education Connections for School, Home and Community.* Port Chester, NY: National Professional Resources, Inc., 2002.

Wolfe, Patricia. *Brain Matters: Translating Research into Classroom Practice.* Alexandria, VA: ASCD, 2001.

About the Editors

Marc A. Brackett, Ph.D., is a Research Scientist in the Department of Psychology at Yale University. He also is Deputy Director of Yale's Health, Emotion, and Behavior Laboratory and Head of the Emotional Intelligence Unit in the Edward Zigler Center in Child Development and Social Policy. In 2006, he created the first interactive university course for undergraduates at Yale on emotional intelligence. Dr. Brackett is the author, co-author, or editor of over 70 scholarly publications, including five educational curricula. His research focuses primarily on the measurement of emotional skills in children and adults; the mechanisms by which emotional skills relate to social competence, mental health, and academic performance, as well as the effects of emotional literacy training on children and adults' personal and professional lives. He has been the principal investigator on many grant-funded projects examining the effects of emotional literacy training in school children, including a multi-million dollar grant from the W.T. Grant Foundation. He is a member of the Research Advisory Board and Program Provider Group at CASEL. Over the last five years Dr. Brackett has trained thousands of teachers and administrators with the goal of creating Emotionally Literate School Districts throughout the world. He also holds a 5th degree black belt in Hapkido, a Korean martial art.

Dr. Janet Pickard Kremenitzer has been in the fields of Education and Developmental Psychology for over 35 years, and has earned two Master Degrees and a Doctorate from Columbia University. Dr. Kremenitzer has had the unique experience of being the Educational Founder of the Maimonides Academy of Connecticut and having developed from its inception, in 1978, this outstanding infant to 6th grade model day school which was a forerunner of the Charter School movement. Social-emotional skills have been a significant part of the integrated curriculum and are a key component of this highly acclaimed institution. Currently she is an Assistant Professor in the Department of Early Childhood and Childhood Education at Lehman College, City University of New York. She also serves as a faculty member (honorary designation) at the Edward Zigler Center in Child Development and Social Policy Yale University and has been an Associate Researach Scientist in the Department of Psychology and the Yale Child Study Center as well as a Research Affiliate to Peter Salovey in the Department of Psychology. Her original line of research was in visual pursuit tracking of newborn infants and she was part of the competent infant research movement of the 70's that helped define the earliest volitional behaviors in humans and the quality of infant early perceptual and related emotional experiences. Dr. Kremenitzer's current research is in emotional intelligence/literacy in both pre-service and in-service teachers as well as emotional literacy of children. She has integrated the *Diary of Anne Frank* into an Aesthetic Emotional Intelligence Curriculum for inner city elementary children and their teachers in collaboration with the Anne Frank Center

USA where she contributes as the Scholar in Residence. She has published numerous articles in teacher education journals and presents regularly at both national and international conferences. She has two grown children, Becky and David, from whom she has over the years learned the most about childhood development, education, and emotional intelligence.

Marvin Maurer began his career as a middle school teacher in upstate New York. Throughout the last 30 years, Mr. Maurer has developed and implemented programs pertaining to the role of emotions and their importance in the learning process. In the early 70s, he created "The Little People Feeling Words Curriculum," the predecessor program to Emotional Literacy in the Classroom. In addition, as a presenter for the New York State Department of Education, Mr. Maurer championed the need for affective education with traditional curriculum. He also designed the first gifted program for the Monticello, NY school system and has worked as a learning disabilities consultant, a university professor, and a private practitioner. Mr. Maurer has retired from teaching but maintains a private practice of clients with whom he uses many strategies of the Emotional Literacy programs.

Marilyn D. Carpenter serves as founder and senior partner for Quest Education, an educational consulting company specializing in learning, instruction, and professional development. She is an emotional literacy program consultant and has provided numerous trainings throughout the United States and abroad. Formerly, she was an assistant professor in the School of Education at the University of Arkansas at Monticello. Ms. Carpenter received her bachelor's degrees in elementary and secondary education from the University of Arkansas at Monticello. She received her elementary and secondary master's degrees and her doctorate in educational administration from the University of Arkansas in Fayetteville. Her experiences as an elementary, middle, high school teacher, K-12 principal, assistant superintendent, and college professor have exposed her to all levels of education.

Susan E. Rivers is an Associate Research Scientist in the Health, Emotion and Behavior Laboratory at Yale University's Department of Psychology, where she also earned her Ph.D. in 2005. Her research focuses on emotional development and the role emotion knowledge and skills play in effective social and intrapersonal functioning in children and adults. Along with Dr. Marc Brackett, Dr. Rivers developed the RULER model of emotional literacy, which posits that recognizing, understanding, labeling, expressing and regulating emotions effectively is critical to optimal development. Dr. Rivers has published several articles and chapters on these topics and is the co-author of school-based curricula that teach emotional literacy to children. She is currently a co-investigator on a major grant, funded by the W.T. Grant Foundation, to evaluate the effectiveness of the emotional literacy curriculum for upper elementary school in a randomized controlled study. She is also a consultant to schools in both the US and abroad and develops children's television programming.

Nicole A. Elbertson is a Research Associate, and the Coordinator of the Health, Emotion, and Behavior Laboratory in the Department of Psychology at Yale University. Nicole works primarily on the development and implementation of emotional literacy programs and the dissemination of information and research related to the programs. She specializes in developing protocols for school districts to enhance the quality of implementation of emotional literacy programs. Additionally, she has worked on studies to promote health behaviors such as smoking cessation, fruit and vegetable consumption, mammography use, and clinical trial participation among cancer patients. Ms. Elbertson is a co-author of numerous research publications in these areas.

Want to join the hundreds of schools that have already adopted
The RULER Approach to Social and Emotional Learning?

Just visit our website: **www.therulerapproach.org**
to learn how to bring our evidence-based Leadership, Educator, Student,
and Family emotional literacy programs to your school.

You can also follow us on Facebook and Twitter by searching for
The RULER Approach.